The Social Anxiety Workbook

THE SOCIAL ANXIETY WORKBOOK

An Hachette UK Company
www.hachette.co.uk

Vie Books, an imprint of Summersdale Publishers Ltd
Part of Octopus Publishing Group Limited
Carmelite House
50 Victoria Embankment
LONDON
EC4Y 0DZ
UK

www.summersdale.com

Printed and bound in China

ISBN: 978-1-83799-336-9

Substantial discounts on bulk quantities of Summersdale books are available to corporations, professional associations and other organizations. For details contact general enquiries: telephone: +44 (0) 1243 771107 or email: enquiries@summersdale.com.

The Social Anxiety Workbook

PRACTICAL TIPS AND GUIDED EXERCISES TO HELP YOU OVERCOME **SOCIAL ANXIETY**

MITA MISTRY

Disclaimer

Neither the author nor the publisher can be held responsible for any injury, loss or claim – be it health, financial or otherwise – arising out of the use, or misuse, of the suggestions made herein. This book is not intended as a substitute for the medical advice of a doctor or physician. If you are experiencing problems with your physical or mental health, it is always best to follow the advice of a medical professional.

Contents

Introduction

Welcome to *The Social Anxiety Workbook*, a guide to understanding and dealing with this condition so that you can work towards a stress-free, confident life.

Starting a self-help journey can be a little scary for anyone, but it's also the most positive first step. So, congratulations to you for picking up this book and taking a proactive action toward improving your well-being.

It's normal for us all to feel out of control when life gets a little bumpy and throws challenges our way, especially when we're cruising along and least expect it. Life can be stressful. We have so much to juggle: balancing family, friendships, work pressures, socializing, online notifications or just everyday stuff – it's hardly surprising we struggle.

When our batteries are running on empty, we're unlikely to feel at our best, and of course, the last thing we might feel we need is to see people. Or if we've been bullied, embarrassed or let down by people in the past, it's understandable to be put off some social situations. But when avoiding one or two social situations turns into long-term anxiety, everyday interactions can feel overwhelming.

The good news is, by learning proven techniques and trying out affirmations, journalling and nourishing activities based on mindfulness and Cognitive Behavioural Therapy (CBT), you will be armed with a toolbox of social-anxiety-busting techniques to help you feel at ease in social situations.

How to Use This Book

This workbook will help you understand how your thoughts, feelings and actions are connected and contribute to social anxiety. You will learn about the impact of social anxiety on your well-being and life. Living with social anxiety can be challenging, but it doesn't have to be this way.

We all go through times when our social battery is low, but we have the power to choose our response. The more we learn about ourselves, the easier it is to find healthy strategies to cope with social anxiety, which boosts our confidence. By picking up this workbook, you've already taken a significant and positive step forward.

You have the strength to break the cycle of worry, and this guide will show you how to do just that. By reframing how you think and exploring techniques to soothe anxious emotions, you can regain a sense of control when facing challenging social situations. You'll be shown how to confront your fears and harness the power of self-care too. This guide will be there for you every step of the way to help you break free from social anxiety. Let's do this!

Who Is This Book For?

This book is for you if you overthink or feel distressed about:

Meeting new people

Speaking with authority figures (e.g. teachers, doctors)

Being the centre of attention

Not being good enough

People watching you eat, drink or fill in forms

Speaking on the phone or on video calls

Being ignored in a group

Emailing people you don't know well

Text messages coming across as dull

Feeling lonely

Speaking in front of people

Returning purchases

Parties or social gatherings

Talking to someone you find attractive

Not feeling confident

Speaking up

Posting on social media

The more of these situations you relate to, the more socially anxious you are likely to be. Even if you only agree with some of the statements on the list, advice from this workbook will still be valuable. With a little support and self-belief, you'll discover ways to calm unpleasant feelings and learn new tools to boost your confidence too. So keep reading – you have nothing to lose and so much to gain!

PART 1

Social Anxiety and You

WHAT IS
SOCIAL ANXIETY?

According to the World Health Organization (WHO), anxiety disorders affect over 300 million people globally, of which social anxiety is one of the most common types. It's when a person has an overwhelming fear of social situations – often manifesting as apprehension regarding potential judgement and feeling socially awkward or paranoid about doing something embarrassing in front of people – coupled with a strong desire to make a positive impression.

It's perfectly normal for many of us, including the most confident individuals, to feel nervous before speaking in front of a group of people or to feel a little uneasy before a date or party. But some people grapple with anxiety in nearly *all* social scenarios – from phone conversations to attending classes or even meeting friends. This heightened sensitivity is often indicative of social anxiety.

Social anxiety, or social phobia, goes beyond shyness or nervousness. It involves intense fear of group situations that hinders enjoyment and participation in everyday life. It can be limited to specific situations or impact various aspects of life, such as work, school and relationships.

What causes
social anxiety?

A little bit of anxiety in social situations is perfectly normal and can motivate us to perform well in front of a group, or protect us from situations which may harm us. This "fight-or-flight" response system has been with us since prehistoric times and it serves to protect us – it's what makes our brains marvellous at spotting all the things that could possibly go wrong. But this negative bias can overshadow all the good things in our life and keep us feeling edgy or down.

Research tells us that people with social anxiety have an overactive amygdala, the fear centre in the brain, which heightens anxiety in group situations. Sometimes the amygdala sees situations as threatening even when they're not.

Social anxiety can be influenced by family history and past experiences, but it's unclear whether it's learned behaviour or genetics. Stressful experiences, like harsh judgement, criticism or bullying, can contribute to a fear of judgement and a lack of confidence. This fear can lead to withdrawal and feelings of loneliness, making it challenging to express our natural friendliness. Others may perceive people with social anxiety as distant or aloof, when in reality they are simply afraid and seeking safety in social interactions.

What does social anxiety sound, feel and look like?

Social anxiety is a self-perpetuating cycle that begins with negative thoughts about social situations, leading to self-doubt and fear. This, in turn, influences your body's response and the safety behaviours you adopt, such as scrolling on your phone to avoid eye contact or someone striking up a conversation.

Imagine you've been invited to a party where you won't know many people.

Social anxiety thoughts and beliefs sound like:

Before party

I'll get it wrong

I'm rubbish at making conversation

I may blush or get sweaty

What if they think I'm awkward?

I'll stumble on my words

I won't fit in

During party

I can't think of what to say

I'm blushing and shaking; they can see I'm anxious

They're talking about me

I sound boring

Everyone is looking at me and judging me

I'm not good enough

After party

I sounded silly

I'm a failure

I made a fool of myself

I can't handle group situations

I looked awkward and nervous

Social anxiety feels like:

Shortness of breath

Racing heart or palpitations

Shaking or trembling

Blushing

Sweating

A choking feeling

Feeling sick or upset stomach

Headache

Tightness in your chest

Hot flushes or chilling feeling

Blurred vision

Dry throat and mouth

Feeling dizzy or lightheaded

Lump in throat

Shaky voice

Tingling or muscles tensing

Numbness

Social anxiety behaviour looks like:

Rehearsing conversations in advance

Cancelling plans

Using social media to replace real-life connection.

Not speaking up in groups or classes

Staying out of the limelight

Finding excuses to leave early

Saying no to invites

Sitting near the exit to escape

Relying on the comfort of friends or family to go to events

Being afraid to ask questions when unsure

Not taking part in social activities (avoidance) or engaging in social activities but relying on safe people or props to make you feel comfortable – like sticking to your best friend or sitting at the back of the room where no one will see you (safety behaviours) – are unhelpful and can make social anxiety worse.

If any of this sounds familiar, then you're experiencing a normal part of social anxiety.

What does social anxiety look, sound and feel like for you?

Think of a time when you felt worried, anxious or afraid. What did your thoughts sound like? How did it feel inside your body? What actions did you take – how did you react? Reflect on the prompts using examples from the previous pages or add your own, and write it all down here:

I think...	I feel...	I react by...

MY SOCIAL ANXIETY

What makes you feel anxious? Perhaps it's a specific situation you go out of your way to avoid because it fills you with dread, or a thought that keeps you up all night worrying. It could be everyday interactions or meeting certain people that worries you.

By writing it all down you create a safe space where you can open up to explore your thoughts and feelings. Writing also helps to lighten heavy thoughts, so you have more headspace. Here are some prompts to help you work through anxiety – remember, be as honest as you can with yourself.

Social situations

Write down any social situations which trigger negative thoughts or fear.

Example thought: I am anxious about meeting new people and worry about saying something ridiculous.

....

....

....

Negative thoughts

Write down any negative thoughts you have about what people will think of you and how you will come across.

Example thought: I am afraid of being judged as awkward or sounding boring because I'm rubbish at making conversations.

....

....

....

....

....

....

....

....

....

....

Safety behaviours

The next step is to understand how your actions are affected when social anxiety is triggered. What avoidance and safety behaviours do you use?

Example actions: I cancel plans or decline invites to avoid social events or, if I do go, I don't start any conversations and make excuses to leave early.

....

....

....

....

....

....

....

....

Symptoms

Now think about which symptoms bother you the most or you think people will notice the most. They could be symptoms that affect how you feel, such as feeling overwhelmed or your mind going blank, or physical symptoms, such as a shaky voice or a racing heart. Jot them down here:

Example symptoms: Speaking with new people makes me blush, feel sweaty and short of breath. This makes me feel embarrassed and self-conscious.

....

....

....

....

....

....

It's helpful to be aware of what you think about yourself so you can learn how
to challenge and reframe unhelpful thoughts. You can explore strategies later in
this workbook.

Negative images

What negative images do you believe about yourself?

Example thought: I am not good enough, everyone is more confident and has
their act together. My whole face turns red when I blush, everyone can see I'm a
nervous wreck.

....

....

....

....

....

Life impact

The next step is to reflect on what impact social anxiety is having on your well-being and life – is it creeping into everyday interactions, or stopping you doing the things you love? In what way has social anxiety held you back recently?

Example: I missed out on seeing a movie at the cinema I really wanted to see because my safe person was unavailable. I was afraid to ask anyone else to join me in case they said no.

....

....

....

Ideal outcome

Finally, reflect on what your ideal outcome would look like if anxiety were released for each situation. Setting a goal to work toward is important because it motivates you and helps you to see your progress.

Example outcome: To feel confident speaking up and enjoy meeting new people. Being able to attend and fully enjoy a friend's birthday celebration without fear of judgement.

....

....

....

Stay hopeful

Hope is being able to see that there is light despite all of the darkness.

DESMOND TUTU

As you've seen, when social anxiety strikes, it's a vicious cycle that can easily spiral out of control. This can leave you feeling like you're sinking, with no solution in sight. When hope is lost, you lose motivation to change. But this cycle can be broken through understanding your anxiety and identifying the many ways you can help yourself – you've already taken a superb step to do just that.

When heavy and painful thoughts take over, and you're struggling to feel positive, even taking one action from this workbook plants a seed of hope – you're moving forward. Don't forget, there is always hope and it is entirely possible for pain to pass.

Keep building on your progress, and if changes don't happen quickly that's okay – keep going, change will inevitably come. Be kind and patient with yourself because we all have good and bad days and that's fine too. Every day is an opportunity for a fresh start. By celebrating your wins, no matter how small, your confidence will grow. Keep working towards your ideal outcome; the next pages are with you every step of the way. You've got this!

PART 2

Dealing with Social Anxiety

Now that you're starting to understand your social anxiety better, and the impact it has on your life, it's time to gently let it go. Sometimes a little anxiety is perfectly normal, but when it starts interfering with your daily life, it becomes problematic.

In order to grow, you have to let go of the unhelpful patterns you've become used to. It's time to change the story and show anxiety who is boss! You will feel so much more in control of your life when you learn strategies to loosen social anxiety's grip on you.

Remember, there isn't a quick fix that will magically improve everything overnight. But take comfort in knowing that you've already taken the crucial initial stride and brighter days are ahead. In this chapter, we'll explore the best ways to tackle unhelpful thoughts and feelings, especially when anxiety takes hold. So let's dive in and discover the tools and techniques that will help you break free.

TACKLING SOCIAL ANXIETY

CBT is a highly effective practical tool that focuses on three key aspects of social anxiety:

1. Our thoughts: This involves questioning anxious situations and reshaping worrisome thoughts into more helpful ones.

2. Our emotions: This entails gaining a better understanding of anxiety symptoms and learning strategies to manage them, empowering us to soothe ourselves when anxiety creeps in.

3. Our actions: This involves breaking free from negative cycles by confronting the things we tend to avoid. It's about taking positive action and showing anxiety who's in charge!

All three are connected and the goal is to escape the cycle of worrying thoughts, as illustrated in the diagram below:

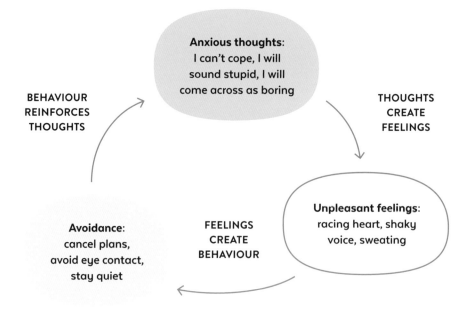

Anxious thoughts: I can't cope, I will sound stupid, I will come across as boring

BEHAVIOUR REINFORCES THOUGHTS

THOUGHTS CREATE FEELINGS

Unpleasant feelings: racing heart, shaky voice, sweating

Avoidance: cancel plans, avoid eye contact, stay quiet

FEELINGS CREATE BEHAVIOUR

Moving on to a more helpful, balanced and positive cycle:

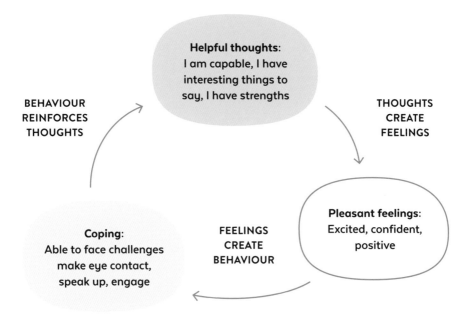

BEHAVIOUR
REINFORCES
THOUGHTS

Helpful thoughts:
I am capable, I have interesting things to say, I have strengths

THOUGHTS
CREATE
FEELINGS

Coping:
Able to face challenges make eye contact, speak up, engage

FEELINGS
CREATE
BEHAVIOUR

Pleasant feelings:
Excited, confident, positive

Truthfully, nobody is completely anxiety-free, not even those zen-like people who glide through life effortlessly. But it is entirely possible to deal with social anxiety by developing healthy coping strategies. After all, anxiety isn't all bad – it motivates us to keep moving in the right direction and accomplish incredible things. Most importantly, it's there to keep us safe from real danger. We just don't want it to constantly trouble us.

Brain dump

Let's explore what's bothering you right now and start to let go of some of your worries by doing a brain dump – writing down everything that's churning through your mind. It's a way to work through your worries and have a little rant to free up headspace.

   Using the prompts to help you get started, write down everything that's bugging you. Perhaps write your thoughts on a separate piece of paper, then you can scrunch them up and throw them in a real bin – you might find the physical act of throwing your worries in the trash quite cathartic!

I can't stop thinking about...

....

....

I'm worried about...

....

....

....

....

....

....

....

....

....

....

....

....

....

....

I'm afraid of...

. . . .

. . . .

. . . .

. . . .

. . . .

. . . .

. . . .

. . . .

I feel under pressure to...

. . . .

. . . .

. . . .

. . . .

. . . .

. . . .

. . . .

I'm so sick of...

....
....
....
....
....
....
....
....

I wish I could change...

....
....
....
....
....
....
....

Calm brain, anxious brain

Our brains possess a survival instinct, triggering the fight-or-flight response to safeguard us. Sometimes, even in non-threatening situations like public speaking, our brain reacts as if we're being chased by a bear, entering "survival" mode.

The problem is this fight-or-flight response impairs our thinking brain's functioning, which is why anxiety can leave us feeling mentally foggy, unable to concentrate or stumbling over words.

Thankfully, the brain is adaptable. So, with a little practice, you can strengthen your thinking brain and switch off survival mode when it's unnecessary. Keep reading on to see how.

- The **thinking brain** handles communication, problem-solving and cognitive tasks. It temporarily shuts down during the fight-or-flight response – after all, writing an email is not a priority when danger is present.

- The **survival brain** protects your vital functions: heart rate, breathing, body temperature, sleep–wake cycles and movement.

- The **emotional brain** serves as a warning system, swiftly guiding you to respond to potential threats.

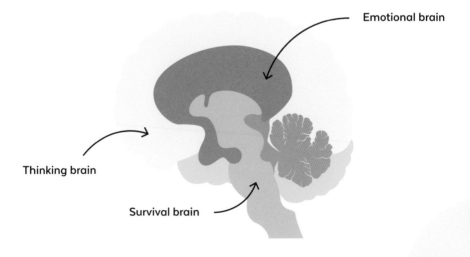

Emotional brain

Thinking brain

Survival brain

Let's explore your calm and anxious brain. When calm, your mind may resemble a flowing river or a serene blue sky over an undisturbed ocean.

When anxious, are there multiple thoughts in your mind like endless open browser tabs? Does it feel foggy or blurred, like thoughts spinning on a merry-go-round? Use the prompts in the table below to delve into your experience, and write your answers in the space provided.

Calm brain	Anxious brain
When my mind is clear, I feel…	When I'm worried, my mind feels…
The things that help me to feel calm are…	Anxiety makes me think…
To feel relaxed, I think about…	Anxiety makes my head feel…

FEEL YOUR FEELINGS

When you're anxious about meeting new people or how you'll be perceived, unpleasant emotions arise from the amygdala, the emotional alarm bell. Instead of pushing uncomfortable feelings away, embrace and acknowledge them (like an annoying yet well-meaning sibling!).

By naming how you feel, you switch on your thinking brain. This helps you to regain control as well as soothe your body and mind.

Take a deep breath and guide yourself through the feeling like this:

I feel anxious.

I'm experiencing awkwardness, nervousness and queasiness before the event, but these feelings won't ruin it.

Anxiety is just a feeling. I am safe and in control.

What is anxiety trying to tell me?

Anxiety is signalling that people might judge me and that I won't succeed at work. While that's possible, I can't predict the future or control others' reactions.

If it happens, I'll handle it.

I can name how my body feels: dry mouth, sweaty palms, racing heart.

I am safe to think and feel this way; anxiety cannot harm me.

This too shall pass.

> Our anxiety does not come from thinking about the future, but from wanting to control it.
>
> KAHLIL GIBRAN

Thoughts and feelings can sometimes get tangled up. Thoughts are the words we tell ourselves, while feelings are the emotions or physical sensations in our bodies. Feeling your emotions as and when they arise helps to prevent outbursts and build better connections.

To honour your body's needs and ease physical symptoms of anxiety, try the following:

1. Sitting comfortably, gently close your eyes and take three deep breaths, filling your lungs.

2. Place one hand over your heart and feel its beat. Place your other hand on your belly and notice how it rises and falls with each breath.

3. Continue breathing deeply and focus on the sound of your inhalations and exhalations.

4. Tune into your body. Can you hear or sense what it's telling you? Is there discomfort, tension, restlessness, fatigue, heat, cold or thirst? Open your eyes at your own pace.

Can you meet your body's needs? Try these techniques if you're experiencing uncomfortable feelings:

- **Tension**: Stretch your body with simple yoga poses, take deep breaths and slowly roll your shoulders and head to release tension.

- **Restlessness**: Go for a brisk walk. Even a 10-minute stroll can help shake off restlessness.

- **Feeling hot or cold**: Hydrate with a glass of water or herbal tea and adjust your clothing layers accordingly.

- **Tired**: Take a break, have a 20-minute nap or plan to get to sleep earlier at night.

Take a deep breath

Purposefully taking deep breaths regularly can calm your anxious brain and ease physical symptoms. Practise diaphragmatic breathing by filling your belly with air like a balloon, then exhaling. Do this exercise for 3 minutes, three times every day for better results.

1. Sit on a comfortable chair or lie on a bed. Close your eyes or soften your gaze. Relax your jaw and breathe slowly (we tend to breathe faster when anxious).

2. Breathe in deeply for a count of four (through your nose).

3. Hold your breath for a count of two.

4. Breathe out for a count of six (through your mouth like a huge sigh of relief).

Set reminders in your phone or diary to breathe three times a day. Use the tracker to record your progress and jot down any notes.

Day	Breath 1	Breath 2	Breath 3	Comments/observations
Week 1				
Monday				
Tuesday				
Wednesday				
Thursday				
Friday				
Saturday				
Sunday				

Day	Breath 1	Breath 2	Breath 3	Comments/observations
Week 2				
Monday				
Tuesday				
Wednesday				
Thursday				
Friday				
Saturday				
Sunday				

Day	Breath 1	Breath 2	Breath 3	Comments/observations
Week 3				
Monday				
Tuesday				
Wednesday				
Thursday				
Friday				
Saturday				
Sunday				

Visualize calm

If your thoughts impact your emotions and actions, it's natural that negative thoughts can lead to sadness and avoidance. The opposite is also true: positive thoughts can promote relaxation and motivation. Try this visualization to calm anxiety:

Look around you. What do you notice in your surroundings? Find the small details, like colours and shapes (blue sky or golden beach).

What sounds can you hear? Are they near or far? Soft or loud? Listen closely to everything, such as birds or crashing waves.

What are you eating or drinking? Are you enjoying it? Does it taste sweet, salty or sour? Take a moment to appreciate the flavours.

What can you feel? Notice how the air feels on your skin, how your clothes feel on your body. Is it hot, cool or warm? Take all the sensations in.

What scents do you notice? What does the air smell like? Are there any fragrances, like seaweed or flowers? Immerse yourself in this nourishing place.

Calm colouring

Research shows that colouring mandalas can relieve social anxiety more than free drawing. They are often used in art therapy as well. Colouring mandalas involves repetitive hand movements and focused attention, providing an escape from bothersome thoughts. It creates a sense of safety, control and familiarity, which is the opposite of what you feel when anxious.

Get a colouring book, download mandalas for free online, or create your own! Sit comfortably, breathe slowly and focus on the shapes and patterns as you colour. Have fun!

Get moving

When anxiety makes you feel tense, movement can be your best ally. It shifts negative energy, promotes relaxation and rewires your brain. Don't let anxiety confine you, just move your body – even if you engage in activities for only 15 minutes. You could try:

Playing your favourite music

Dancing

Walking mindfully, taking in your surroundings

Gardening

Jogging around the block

Brisk walking

Cycling to the local shop or work

Stretching

Yoga

What movement can you do today for 15 minutes? Be spontaneous and, most importantly, be led by whatever rhythm feels good for you.

Take care of your body. It's the only place you have to live.

JIM ROHN

MIND GAMES

Stepping out of your comfort zone can trigger stress and anxiety. Whether it's leading a group discussion or meeting new people, our minds can overreact to unusual situations. But don't worry! You can use discreet and easy tricks to distract yourself from those uncomfortable thoughts and feelings. Experiment with these techniques to find what works best for you:

- Count backwards from 100.
- Recite a poem or the alphabet.
- Count all the red cars on the road.
- Think of an object, such as an animal, and "draw" it in your mind, or in the air with your finger.
- Think of foods that begin with the letter P.
- Make up a silly joke – the kind you'd find in a sweet wrapper. It may make you laugh too!
- Name as many fruits as you can.
- Pick up an object and describe its colour, texture, size, weight and scent.
- Describe your surroundings using all five senses.

Make your own list of go-to distraction tools.

....

....

....

....

Mindful breathing

Mindful breathing calms anxious thoughts by shifting focus, activating the parasympathetic nervous system and reducing stress hormones.

1. Sitting comfortably, gently close your eyes. Feel the weight of your body on your chair as you allow it to become still. Take a few deep breaths. Relax your shoulders, face muscles, hands and legs. Let go of all tension in your body.

2. Notice your breathing and what the air feels like as it comes into your nose, goes down your throat into your lungs and then back out through the nose. Observe your stomach rising and falling. Allow your breathing to be relaxed and natural without trying to change it in any way. You are simply being, complete and whole in this moment. If your mind wanders, gently guide it back to your breath.

3. Imagine the most beautiful mountain you've ever seen. It might reach into the sky or have soft peaks. Know that this mountain has a large base rooted in the earth. Notice how solid, strong and unmoving it is. Perhaps your mountain has waterfalls trickling down the slopes or snow on the peaks. Focus on this image.

4. Notice how the mountain remains solid and still, regardless of seasonal changes like heavy winter snowfall, spring showers, summer heat or autumn winds. In the same way, we can learn to experience tranquillity in the face of storms in our lives. Feel the stillness of the mountain, knowing you can visit this place any time.

5. Gently open your eyes.

Pro tip: **Try this outdoors. Let the sounds and scents of nature soothe you.**

Quick calm-down tools

If you can't stop thinking about worst-case scenarios happening (like everyone talking behind your back), you can stop those pesky thoughts in their tracks before anxiety spirals out of control. Grounding techniques do just that. Experiment with these techniques and choose some to add to your toolbox:

1. Name five things you can see, four things you can feel, three things you can hear, two things you can smell and one thing you can taste. Keep a small snack or gum handy for the taste.

2. Stamp your feet on the ground and focus on the sensations in your feet and legs. Remember, your feet are firmly grounded.

3. Engage your sense of touch by holding something solid, like your phone or house key. Pay attention to its temperature, shape and texture to slow racing thoughts.

4. Seek comfort by hugging someone you trust or petting an animal. It releases oxytocin, the feel-good hormone.

5. Create a go-to calming playlist on your phone. Listen to soothing beats or nature sounds. Alternatively, take a break and listen to a funny podcast to pause overwhelming thoughts.

Thoughts and feelings diary

Keep a thoughts and feelings diary to identify your triggers and note soothing strategies for coping with social anxiety. Record every time you feel anxious and reflect on patterns. Use the example provided below and create additional sheets if needed. Learn from each entry to better understand your experiences.

Date	Situation	What did you feel?	What thoughts did you have?	How did you respond?
14 Dec	Talking to cashier	Racing heart, dizziness, dry mouth	I'm rubbish at small talk, she thinks I'm awkward	Rushed out of store, had a fizzy drink to cool down

Date	Situation	What did you feel?	What thoughts did you have?	How did you respond?

My warning signs

When anxiety strikes, your body undergoes uncomfortable changes. However, anxiety cannot harm you. With practice, you can control these sensations. Recognizing your warning signs helps you apply healthy coping strategies. Circle anxiety symptoms you experience and add your own if you wish. Think about which strategies make you feel in control.

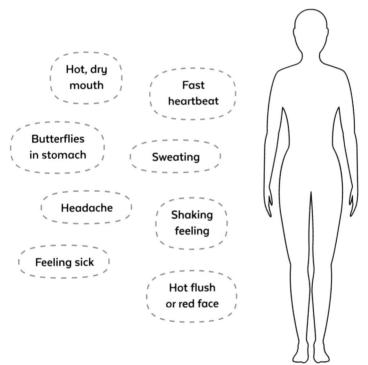

Hot, dry mouth

Fast heartbeat

Butterflies in stomach

Sweating

Headache

Shaking feeling

Feeling sick

Hot flush or red face

Using a different colour for each emotion, colour in each square and the part of your body where you feel that emotion.

☐ Sadness   ☐ Fear   ☐ Anger   ☐ Rage

My positive self

Do you worry that people secretly find you boring or that everyone else is more interesting? Comparing ourselves to others can chip away at our self-esteem and fuel social anxiety. Negative thoughts reinforce the idea that we are not good enough, and this rut stops us from embracing positive experiences as our brains are fixated on finding problems. To counteract this habit, pause and reflect on past enjoyable experiences.

What is a positive social situation that I've had recently?

Describe a time when you felt confident. Where were you? What were you doing?

What qualities do you like about yourself?

Write a list of nice things people say about you.

PART 3

Overcoming Negative Thoughts

In the last chapter, we explored valuable techniques to help you cope better every day. On those extra-tough days, give yourself a little more kindness. Revisit your positive self on page 47 to remind you that you are good enough and you are just as interesting and worthy of love as everyone else.

Now that you understand how social anxiety affects your mind, body and actions, let's dig a *little* deeper into dealing with those negative thoughts that hold you back from being yourself. Annoying thoughts, be gone!

In this chapter, you'll discover the art of confronting your negative thoughts, rectifying thinking errors and dispelling unhelpful beliefs about yourself. This process will usher in a sense of increased confidence and relaxation, which you totally deserve. You're doing an amazing job so far. So keep going – these pages are here to support you and cheer for your success. Let's do this!

Thoughts are not facts

Our minds generate around 70,000 automatic thoughts daily, which demonstrates the brilliance of our brains. Unfortunately, in the interests of our survival and to keep us safe, most of these thoughts tend to be negative. Social anxiety is associated with increased negative thinking.

Negative automatic thoughts fuel worst-case scenarios. For instance, when entering a room full of people, thoughts like, "Everyone will judge me" or "No one will like me" may arise. Once caught up in negativity, it's difficult to stop these ideas spiralling out of control. These thoughts sow seeds of doubt that grow with each ounce of attention we give them.

Let's clarify one thing: OUR THOUGHTS ARE NOT FACTS, nor are they consistently accurate. However, thoughts hold power as they influence our emotions and behaviours. We all tend to overthink and jump to conclusions without complete information, like assuming we upset a friend who didn't reply to a message when they were simply busy.

Unhelpful thoughts and thinking traps bring us down. So the next time an irritating thought surfaces, such as "You'll always be awkward", remind yourself it's merely an annoying noise and assert, "Nice try, you're not a fact!"

One of our greatest freedoms is how we react to things.

CHARLIE MACKESY

Know your thoughts

Negative thoughts are incredibly damaging to your self-esteem, self-worth and confidence. They need to go! To overcome them, you must start by identifying them. Psychologists and therapists suggest that understanding your thoughts is highly beneficial, so let's get curious and explore. Take a moment to review your thoughts and feelings diary (page 44) or recall a situation that made you anxious. Write them down like this:

What situation makes you anxious?	What are your feelings?	What are your thoughts?
Going out to a bar	Heart racing, dry mouth	I don't fit in
Friend is ignoring me	Rejected, sad, alone	I'm invisible

Negative-thought catcher

It takes practice to catch the thoughts that make you anxious, but you're doing great – keep going.

Pay attention to changes in your anxiety. When you notice yourself feeling more anxious, ask yourself:

What am I thinking right now?

....
....
....
....
....

What is making me feel anxious?

....
....
....
....
....

What am I worried will happen?

....
....
....
....
....

What worst-case scenario do I think will happen?

....
....
....
....
....

Negative thoughts can be words or images. Circle the negative thoughts you experience about social situations.

If any of these thoughts sound familiar, don't worry – read on to see how to deal with them.

You can write your own or draw images of your negative thoughts in the box below.

Thinking traps

Thinking traps are overly negative and unfair ways of seeing things. We all experience these pitfalls but calling them out can be game-changing. Here are some thinking traps and examples. Have you fallen into any of these?

Thinking trap	Example
Personalization	He turned away because I'm boring. She looks angry, probably because she's working with me.
Jumping to conclusions	They're looking at me so they must be talking about me or laughing at me.
Mind-reading or predicting the future	I will always be alone. People think I'm stupid.
Catastrophizing	If something goes wrong, it will be a disaster. I will never be able to show my face at work if it goes badly.
Rejecting positives	Thanks for the compliment, it was luck. I'm not special.
Over-generalizing	I never remember names. I'm always late.
Labelling	I'm an idiot. I can't even hold a conversation.
Magnifying	I messed up in a big way. I'm having a heart attack.
"Should" statements	I should never feel anxious. I should never make mistakes.

Balanced thoughts

Balanced thoughts are like the kind, reassuring friend we all need – someone who is gentle yet gives us a fair perspective. When our thoughts are calm and realistic, as opposed to fear-based worst-case scenarios that trap us, we're more likely to feel safe to connect with others. To create balanced thoughts, you must notice negative ones as soon as they pop up and get better at challenging them before they drag you down. Fight back by asking yourself:

- If my friend had these thoughts, what would I tell them?
- Would I be thinking differently if I was feeling more positive?
- Am I considering all relevant facts about this situation?
- Is there any real evidence?
- Am I ignoring my strengths?
- What's the worst that could happen?
- Would life still go on?
- What's the best that could happen?
- Am I falling into a thinking trap (e.g. mind-reading, jumping to conclusions)?
- Am I 100 per cent certain that it will happen?
- If it did happen, what could I do to cope with it?

Balanced thinking means looking at yourself, others and the world in a fair way. It's a kind and effective way to stop the social anxiety cycle.

The greatest weapon against stress is our ability to choose one thought over another.

WILLIAM JAMES

CHALLENGE YOUR NEGATIVE THOUGHTS

Challenge your negative thoughts and thinking traps by noting down balanced thoughts. Generate as many as you can. Here are a few examples to help you begin:

Thinking trap	What are your feelings?	Balanced thought
Personalization	I don't fit in	People are not judging me.
Jumping to conclusions	She thinks I'm boring.	Maybe I can't tell what she thinks.
Mind-reading or predicting the future	I will not enjoy myself. Everyone will think I'm odd.	It could be fun.
Catastrophizing	If I don't present well, everyone's going to talk about it.	I'm as good as everyone else.
Rejecting positives	It wasn't my best work, I got lucky.	My hard work deserves acknowledgement.
Over-generalizing	I'm always late.	I'm sometimes late but so are most people.
Labelling	I'm an idiot.	I'm capable and have a voice.
Magnifying	I'm having a heart attack.	My heart is racing as I'm anxious, it will pass.
"Should" statements	I should never feel anxious. I should never make mistakes.	Anxiety is normal, my feelings are valid. It's okay to make mistakes and learn from them.

Thinking trap	What are your feelings?	Balanced thought

Best outcome

Anxiety can cause us to overestimate the likelihood of something bad happening and let our mind wander to the worst possible outcome. But if our mind can imagine the worst, it can certainly imagine the best too – both are imaginary! Start challenging the worst and replacing it with the best outcome.

Think of a situation that makes you anxious.
Example: Presenting badly, stumbling on my words and everyone talking about me.
Imagine the situation playing out. Describe the...

Worst possible outcome:

....

....

Best possible outcome:

....

....

Likely outcome:

....

....

A more accurate thought is, "My presentation might be okay, but if I do mess up, everyone will soon forget about it." Remember, most people are too busy worrying about their own problems or looking at their phones!

Be fair to yourself

By now, you've probably noticed your thoughts can be quite harsh. Does your inner dialogue lift you up or tear you down? It's common to experience self-criticism, but when it becomes constant it can really damage your self-esteem. Often, this critical voice stems from childhood and a fear of not being good enough or facing rejection. Unfortunately, many of us were never taught how to silence it.

But here's the good news: you can be fair to yourself. Next time you're feeling down, pay attention to your inner talk. What words do you use? What's the tone like? Does it resemble the criticism of someone from your past? For example, after an event you might say, "You're terrible at socializing."

Now, meet this inner bully with compassion. Imagine speaking kindly to a friend in need. Be encouraging. Say, "I understand you feel awful after the party and believe nobody liked you, but remember, your thoughts are not facts." Speaking kindly creates a sense of safety, like a warm verbal hug.

Above all, remember this: if you wouldn't say it to a friend, don't say it to yourself. Quieting the inner bully requires daily practice, just like any skill. Ask yourself, "Do I want to spend time with my judgemental bully or my kind friend?"

COPING STATEMENTS

On those tough days, look after yourself a little more. Use kind phrases before, during and after a social gathering, such as these coping statements:

Before

- If I get anxious, I will try deep breathing.
- I just need to do my best, that's all I can do.
- People can't tell when I am anxious.
- I have got through this before and I'll get through it again.
- When this feeling passes, I'll be glad I put myself out there.

During

- Other people's behaviour is not always about me.
- Nobody is judging me.
- Not everyone likes everyone and that's okay.
- This feeling is hard, but it will pass soon.
- I do not need to escape or run.

After

- I'm strong for challenging myself to face scary things.
- I will not obsess about how I came across.
- I will not let "what if?" thoughts consume me.
- I refuse to stress about small stuff.
- I choose to distract myself.

Practise self-kindness often by speaking positively about yourself. Change the story and replace self-criticism with affirmations like, "I am capable of handling challenges." Doing so will soothe you and boost your self-esteem. Write your coping statements here:

Coping statements **before** a social gathering	
Coping statements **during** a social gathering	
Coping statements **after** a social gathering	

Mindfulness of thoughts

You've already been introduced to mindfulness (page 42), which is a brilliant technique for stopping pesky thoughts from wreaking havoc in our minds. Mindfulness pauses the negative stories our thoughts tell us. By shining a light on these, we give them less power. We can step back from worst-case scenarios to take a more balanced view.

Science shows that mindfulness positively impacts the thinking and emotional regulation part of our brain and calms the stress response. It keeps us in the present moment and, therefore, less prone to being triggered by worry.

Try noticing your thoughts as though you're watching a film in your mind. The idea is to sit and watch, even though you might feel like pressing mute, stopping or fast-forwarding the film. By watching, you learn to get more comfortable with bothersome thoughts while training your mind to be calmer. Over time, they can't bother you. Amazing!

Don't be pushed by your problems. Be led by your dreams.

RALPH WALDO EMERSON

Try this exercise for 5–10 minutes. There is no right or wrong outcome, just allow your experience to be.

Close your eyes and imagine a cool, calm stream. Water is gently trickling downhill over rocks and around trees. It's a beautiful day with a gentle breeze. The sun's rays warm your face. Every now and then a leaf falls into the water and floats downstream. Imagine you are sitting on the bank watching the leaves drifting by. Every time a thought pops up, imagine it's written on one of them. Stay here and let the thought leaves float by without trying to make the stream flow faster or slower. Notice whatever thoughts or feelings show up and let them be.

Practise this daily and colour how you feel after the exercise on the diagram below:

☐ **Happier**　　☐ **The same**　　☐ **Worse**

Challenge core beliefs

Like negative thoughts, core beliefs shape our self-perception and world view. Negative thinking often stems from these beliefs. People with social anxiety may hold unrealistic beliefs, such as:

- I need to be perfect to be liked.
- I am weak.
- I am unlovable.
- I am a failure.
- The world is dangerous.
- I will end up alone.
- People can't be trusted.
- No one likes me.
- I am worthless.

To challenge a core belief, gather evidence that proves it isn't entirely true. Recall experiences from childhood to the present that contradict the belief. Every piece of evidence counts, even if you're unsure of its relevance. For example, passing a driving test counters the belief of being a failure.

Challenge yourself: if you think you are worthless, boring, socially incompetent, a failure or unlovable, find three pieces of proof that you are not.

Belief	Evidence against it
Example: No one likes me.	1. I receive invites to go out. 2. I have friends. 3. People talk to me.
	1. 2. 3.
	1. 2. 3.
	1. 2. 3.

Uncovering deeply ingrained beliefs can be challenging, but don't worry if it's difficult. You've already made significant progress, and many people seek help from a therapist for this. Trying is superb, so well done – you've got this!

CHANGE THE SPOTLIGHT

People with social anxiety have heightened self-focus, which magnifies worst-case scenarios and the chances of misinterpreting social situations – like that awkward feeling when you're convinced everyone is staring at that stain on your top, but nobody even noticed.

By training your attention, you learn to shift the spotlight away from yourself and onto others, which helps conversations flow and strengthens connections. Start engaging your senses in everyday activities to redirect your focus so you will be able to socialize without excessive worry. Try this:

Noticing your breathing, consider the sensations in your feet while walking. Observe the details in your day: the aroma of food, the water temperature during a shower, the taste of toothpaste. Guide your mind back to the task if it wanders. Practise attention training daily.

Worry often gives a small thing a big shadow.

SWEDISH PROVERB

The beauty of attention training is there's no need to add it to your to-do list. Use these prompts during everyday activities like washing dishes, commuting, eating, getting dressed or making tea. Jot notes on your experience.

Touch: Where on your body do you have contact with the task? Is the texture rough/smooth/hot/cold?	
Smell: What aromas can you smell? How many are there? Are they light/heavy?	
Sight: What do you see? What do you notice about the colours/shadows/shapes/lighting?	
Hearing: What sounds can you hear? Are they loud/soft/near/far?	
Taste: What flavours do you notice? How many are there? Are they overpowering?	

Focus on socializing

Once you've practised attention training, you're ready to use your new skill! When you're in social situations, your aim is to notice when your focus turns inwards and promptly shift it towards making conversation, maintaining eye contact, listening and asking questions. It might sound a little scary – and that's natural. The more you practise, the easier it will get, and your confidence will grow.

When socializing, bear in mind that people may look relaxed even if they don't feel it. Everyone has their own concerns, and their priority isn't looking for flaws or judging you. Like you, most people want positive interactions and are not entirely happy with how they come across. Remember, you don't have to take responsibility to keep a conversation going – moments of silence are perfectly normal and acceptable.

Stay curious, redirect your attention outwards and observe. Notice if other people show signs of nervousness. Have faith that people won't think less of you or dislike you because you're anxious. Would you feel empathy for someone who is feeling anxious? If the answer is yes, other people probably feel the same. Afterwards, avoid carrying out a post-mortem of the situation – try mind games (page 41) or breathing exercises instead.

Social event	What happened – where was your attention, what thoughts and feelings did you have?	What was the outcome? How did you feel afterwards?
Example: Birthday party	I stopped the thought "they think I'm awkward" by asking questions about holidays.	People were excited to share holiday plans. I feel inspired to travel. I feel confident.

Test it out

Because your brain loves evidence, it's helpful to test the accuracy of your thoughts or beliefs. For example, how awful would it be if people saw you blush or tremble, or if you said something silly? We might assume it would be horrible and that we wouldn't cope.

So let's get curious and test this out! Plan to ask an obvious question or say something silly and see what happens. Be mindful not to assume people are reacting negatively – remember, thoughts are not facts.

Here are some experiments to try:

- Make your hand look shaky on purpose to see how people react.
- Ask a "silly" question (e.g. ask for directions to a city you are already in).
- Drop something or knock something over.
- Wear your top or jacket inside out.
- Send a text message with spelling mistakes and random emojis.
- Pretend to forget what you were about to say mid-sentence.
- When sitting at your desk, start humming or singing!

Add your own experiments too.

Review and reflect

Use these prompts to reflect on your experiments.

What happened? What did people say or do?

....

....

....

....

....

....

Was it as bad as you expected?

....

....

....

....

....

....

What could you do differently next time?

....

....

....

....

....

....

PART 4

Boosting Positive Thoughts

Learning to manage social anxiety requires a lot of effort, but it's worth it. Even if you feel you're only making a small amount of progress, it's important to acknowledge and celebrate your achievements. You're doing an amazing job by continuing to work on yourself.

In the last chapter you explored ways to untangle negative thoughts and beliefs. You also learned about the importance of being kind to yourself and finding evidence to prove your mind wrong. Remember to practise these strategies every day.

Now that you're making fabulous progress in breaking the cycle of social anxiety, it's time to increase your positive thoughts. In the next pages, you'll discover tools to work with your strengths, boost your self-esteem, assert yourself and act with confidence in social settings. With every new activity, you'll start to feel more confident in social situations.

Hidden strengths of social anxiety

Social anxiety may seem like a gloomy experience, but that's not the whole story. In fact, socially anxious people have remarkable strengths that are needed in our world now more than ever. Let's take a moment to appreciate these admirable qualities.

Those who struggle with small talk often excel at delving deep into topics they're passionate about. They are empathetic, helpful and considerate of others' feelings, making them fantastic listeners and respected individuals. Their ability to build bridges makes them perfect partners and the best kind of friends. Who doesn't love genuine people?

Consider this: your tendency to think before speaking or sending messages leads to positive first impressions and better relationships. Your built-in warning system enhances your ability to respond to threats, powering your attention to detail. This leads to intelligence, achievement and the creation of outstanding work driven by high standards. It's truly amazing!

Remember, none of us are completely good or bad. If you struggle with social anxiety, recognize it has played a positive and healthy role in shaping who you are and who you're becoming. Perhaps you're the caring friend, the attentive partner, the hardworking colleague, the empathetic leader or the thoughtful sibling. Anxiety doesn't define you; it's simply something that happens, and it happens to many people. It's a normal part of being human that can be both beautiful and a little messy at times, and that's perfectly okay.

Strike a power pose

Power-posing involves standing like a superhero. Studies show expanding your body so that you're taking up space sends signals to your brain to be confident. It makes you feel stronger and more powerful. How can you not feel confident when you're pretending to be a superhero? Try this:

Stand tall as if there is a string of beads from the top of your head to the ceiling, holding your spine upright. Move your feet hip-width apart – notice your feet grounded on the floor. Take a few deep breaths in, then let them out. Place your hands on your hips, point your chin up, roll your shoulders back and puff your chest out. Take up space. Stay in this confident power pose for 2 minutes.

Visualize how being confident will positively impact you and how amazing you'll be at the interview, date or event, for example. When you're ready, bring your hands down. How do you feel?

You can do this at home, at work, outside or anywhere you feel comfortable.

Pro tip: **Watch videos of inspiring icons. Notice their body language – how do they carry themselves? Take inspiration and emulate some of their qualities.**

My strengths and qualities

People who know their strengths and use them frequently have higher self-esteem, better moods and less anxiety. Learning to play to your strengths is something anyone can achieve.

Circle your strengths in the list below, or add your own (yes, you do have them!).

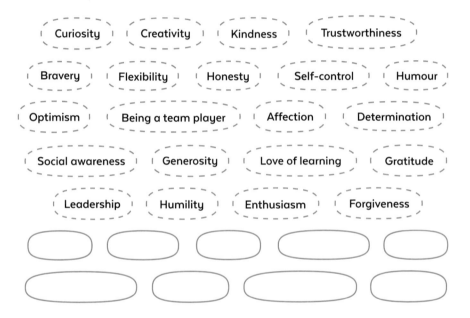

Now, for the next week, write a plan for using your strengths, like the example in the table below:

Day	Strength	Plan
Example	Determination	Practise social skills and talk to people in the office
1		
2		

Day	Strength	Plan
3		
4		
5		
6		
7		

When we're caught up in an anxious rut, it's harder to remember our strengths. Use these prompts to remind you.

Things I am good at...

Compliments I have received...

Challenges I have overcome...

Things that make me unique...

Positive affirmations

Many people find positive affirmations life-changing because they help to relieve anxiety, increase neural pathways in the brain and brighten your outlook. Repeating affirmations to yourself before, during and after social situations is a powerful way to boost your positive thoughts. Try these:

I am not my negative thoughts.

I choose to have meaningful relationships.

I am a confident speaker.

I like being around people.

I can feel anxious and still attend social gatherings.

I do not have to isolate myself.

I can be myself.

I am getting stronger and better every single day.

I am confident and capable of handling social situations.

I am comfortable in my own skin.

I can achieve my goals and dreams.

I have interesting things to say.

Even if you don't believe you are confident, act like it's true and you'll see a difference in social situations.

Write your own personal affirmations. Reframe any negative thoughts such as "I am not confident" or "I can't do it" with a positive empowering statement: "I am capable" or "I can do anything I put my mind to." To ensure this exercise is as transformative as possible, choose something that's easy to remember and means something to you.

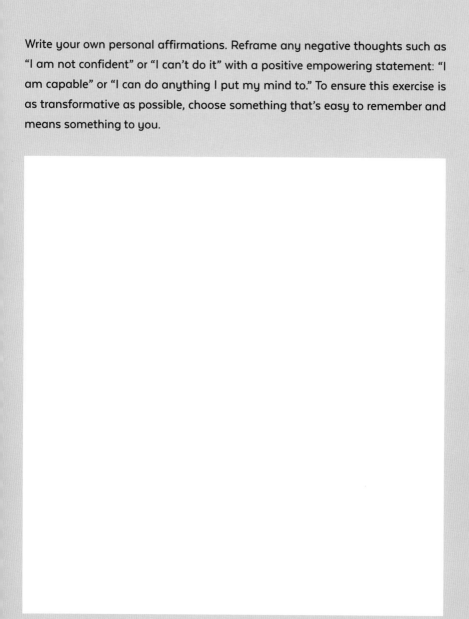

Repeat your affirmations regularly to help reinforce positive thinking.

Assert yourself

Your needs, beliefs and rights are just as important as anyone else's. So it's fine to stand up for what you want and communicate it, as long as you respect other people's needs too. That's what assertiveness looks like.

If you go with the flow or with what everyone else wants and find it hard to say no (which a lot of socially anxious people experience), it's time to practise being more assertive. It's not about disregarding other people; the goal is to negotiate social situations. Try this:

Plan what you are going to say. Use specific sentences. Express your thoughts calmly and take responsibility for your feelings. Use confident body language and maintain eye contact when expressing yourself. Assertive statements can sound like:

- I would like to watch comedy.
- I enjoyed chatting and being heard.
- I feel hurt that you talked about me behind my back.
- I won't be able to go shopping with you, I've had a long week and want to rest.
- I know you're busy, but I feel sad that we don't spend any time together.

See? It doesn't need to be overcomplicated, but you must respect your needs and be direct about them. Once you start asserting yourself regularly, it will feel natural. You can do it!

Social skills supercharge

Taking small, manageable steps to build your social confidence, such as making eye contact with strangers or initiating small talk with acquaintances, can lead to big wins. Every small interaction matters. Try these:

- Say hello to a neighbour – be friendly, wave.
- Call someone you haven't spoken to in a while.
- Say good morning, give a compliment (it lifts you, too).
- Find out one new thing about people you meet (favourite food, hobby, holiday).
- Share something about yourself with a colleague or someone in a queue.
- Accept an invitation to a place you might feel uncomfortable.
- Meet someone for coffee.

Social connection challenge

Think of someone who has supported you or who makes you smile in their presence. It could be a friend or co-worker – or anyone! Write a quick message to them, saying something like:

I was just thinking about you. Thank you for your support. It would be great to catch up over a coffee, phone call or lunch soon.

This might seem a little scary as there is a risk that we don't know how the other person will respond. But think of how you would react to a message like this; the person will probably be delighted to hear from you. It will lift them and you.

FACE YOUR FEARS

You've come a long way in building your confidence! Now it's time to face some fears. Fear is nothing more than an obstacle standing in the way of your progress. By facing your fears, you can move forwards with greater strength and resilience.

Start off with milder sources of anxiety: speaking up more in groups, accepting invites or making more eye contact. Then work up to more challenging situations. By the time you reach the toughest steps, they might not be so anxiety-triggering. Order the following situations as a staircase you are about to climb, with the least challenging step at the bottom and the most at the top:

Most anxious

Offer to lead a team meeting

Say more about myself

Socialize with new people

Have lunch with co-workers

Not scroll on phone to avoid people at events

Say at least two things when in a group or meeting

Reply to group messages and share my ideas

Least anxious

Create your own anxiety staircase here:

Most anxious

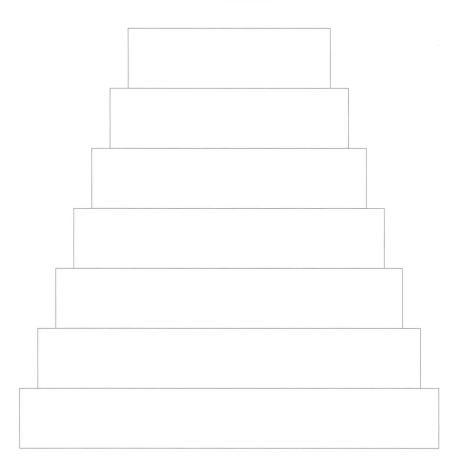

Least anxious

Let's talk

Perhaps you've got an event coming up and you're dreading what to say. It's perfectly okay to prepare some questions beforehand so you feel more in control.

Ideally, let conversations flow naturally and focus on listening to people with genuine interest, but if you do get stuck try asking:

- How do you know the host?
- What's been the highlight of your week?
- What holidays do you have planned?
- Do you have a pet? If not, what pet would you have?
- What books, movies or food have you enjoyed lately?
- What exciting projects are you or will you be working on?
- Which hobbies are you enjoying?

Jot your own questions here:

....

....

....

....

....

....

....

Most people love talking about themselves if someone is willing to listen! But don't forget to share stories about your wonderful self too – you're just as important!

Review and reflect

After completing the experiments, reflect on your experiences. Note your accomplishments, such as speaking in a group, making a new friend, proving a negative thought wrong or feeling more confident.

I accomplished...

....

....

....

....

....

I felt proud when...

....

....

....

....

I would like to build on...

....

....

....

....

....

PART **5**

Taking Care
of Yourself

Now that you've learned some valuable techniques for boosting your confidence, self-esteem and positive thinking, it's time to shift your attention towards self-care.

Achieving good emotional and physical health takes time and effort; it doesn't just magically happen overnight. Fortunately, we often engage in activities that contribute to our mental and physical health without even realizing it. For example: eating well, exercising, getting enough sleep, staying connected with friends and family and spending time outdoors are self-care behaviours which help to build resilience.

It's no big secret that making a conscious effort to practise self-care can improve our well-being, and it's especially important for those of us who are socially anxious. In fact, it's scientifically proven to eliminate or lessen anxiety and depression, reduce stress, improve concentration, calm anger and frustration, boost energy and improve happiness.

Keep pushing forward and tune into the life-enhancing power of self-care. You're well on your way to feeling your most confident and fulfilled self!

What does self-care sound, feel and look like?

Self-care encompasses activities that bring you joy and nourish your mind and body, such as reading a book, getting a haircut, cooking a healthy meal or swimming. It's important to set aside time for self-care rituals and routines in your daily life. They help to structure your day, which, in turn, makes you feel safe and in control by calming your nervous system.

This self-care check-in will help you assess the frequency and effectiveness of your self-care activities, allowing you to identify areas for improvement and better understand your needs. Remember, there's no right or wrong way to practise self-care – you'll find helpful tips throughout the following pages to support your personal needs.

Caring for myself is not self-indulgence, it is self-preservation.

AUDRE LORDE

Look at the table opposite and rate your level of self-care from 1 to 3 for each behaviour.

1	I never or rarely do this
2	I do this okay, sometimes
3	I do this well, often
★	I would like to do even better at this, even more often

	1	2	3	★
Physical self-care				
Eat well				
Eat regularly				
Stay hydrated				
Exercise				
Get enough sleep				
Wear clothes I feel good in				
Rest when tired				
Take care of hygiene (teeth, hair, nails)				
Psychological and emotional self-care				
Immerse myself in hobbies				
Break from distractions (technology, social media)				
Express my feelings healthily (writing, art, talking)				
Recognize my strengths				
Do relaxing things (bath, read, nature, yoga)				
Talk about my problems				
Find reasons to laugh				
Go places (out in nature, coffee shop, new city, holiday)				
Social self-care				
Spend time with people I like				
Stay in touch with friends and family				
Have interesting conversations				
Meet new people				
Do enjoyable activities with people				
Ask for help				
Personal growth				
Learn new things				
Practise gratitude				
Stay true to myself and my values				
Have healthy boundaries				
Spend time reflecting				

What nourishes me?

Now that you're aware of your self-care needs, use the examples below to create a list of what nourishes you and what drains you. Whenever you feel anxious, refer to this list so you can prioritize more feel-good activities and do less of the draining ones.

Nourishing	Draining
Getting eight hours' sleep, taking a brisk walk in nature, cooking a nutritious meal	Reading the news, being in noisy environments, eating junk food

Self-care is about making time every day to work on your mental health and just be. Purposefully add one or two nourishing activities to your daily routine and remove one or two of your draining behaviours.

Spend time reflecting

Make time daily to reflect on your thoughts, behaviours and feelings to help deal with social anxiety. Check in with yourself using these questions:

What was one helpful and one unhelpful thought today?

How helpful were my behaviours?

How did I feel?

What can I do differently tomorrow?

Your feelings are valid. If you're feeling consistently low for six weeks or more, seek help from a doctor or mental health professional. There's no shame in asking for help; it's a sign of strength.

Soothe your senses

Life can get pretty loud. Our senses are bombarded with constant stimulation, from bright lights and screens to notifications, smells and the constant buzz of people chattering. Of course, social anxiety makes things tougher. It heightens your senses, which amplifies sensory overload, causing you to feel more irritable and restless and giving you the urge to escape or panic. To soothe your senses, try:

- **Sound**: Listen to calming music, guided meditation or nature sounds. Sing or hum to yourself, turn off notifications, avoid loud environments.
- **Smell**: Soak up comforting smells, such as scented candles or essential oils, or bake cakes.
- **Taste**: Savour pleasant tastes, such as herbal teas, hot chocolate or your favourite snacks that soothe you. Eat/drink them slowly and mindfully.
- **Touch**: Put on your favourite cosy jumper, touch a blanket or stress ball. Hug someone you trust or cuddle a pet.
- **Sight**: Look at serene photos of loved ones, pets, beaches or sunsets. Watch a feel-good movie, observe flowers or trees.

You could create a self-soothing pack. In a box, put objects or reminders of how to soothe your senses, such as herbal teabags or photos of sunsets. Make a mobile self-soothing toolkit to carry with you.

Eat well

Ever experienced intense hunger pangs or felt jittery and irritable? Most people have felt "hangry" or "hanxious" at some point. Hunger and anxiety have a close but complex relationship – triggering each other and influencing our eating habits.

Studies suggest that certain anxiety-calming foods can benefit brain function and potentially alleviate anxiety symptoms. So the next time you're feeling anxious, pause and ask yourself if you're hungry or thirsty. Prioritize nourishing food over junk food to take care of yourself in the best way.

Best anxiety-calming snacks

- **Legumes**: hummus, lentils
- **Fruits**: apples, strawberries dipped in dark chocolate (a little dark chocolate is good for the brain!)
- **Nuts**: a small handful of almonds with raisins, peanut butter on wholewheat toast, prebiotic yoghurt with nuts
- **Vegetables**: green smoothie (kale or spinach)
- **Spices**: ginger tea, turmeric latte
- **Wholegrains**: wholewheat crackers with smashed avocado
- **Fermented foods**: kefir, kombucha

While it's understandably tempting to reach for comfort foods, they can worsen anxiety. It's best to avoid sugary drinks, chocolate, processed foods, caffeine and alcohol.

STRONG BODY, SERENE MIND

Our bodies love and need exercise, not only for building healthy bones and strong muscles but also to loosen tension and calm our emotions. Exercise releases endorphins – the feel-good brain chemicals which make you feel serene like you're floating on clouds.

The good news is you don't need fancy equipment to start building regular exercise into your schedule. You just need to set aside 10–15 minutes to get those feel-good hormones flowing around your body. Try these exercises at home:

- Walk up and down some stairs. Start off slowly then pick up your speed, being mindful not to slip.
- Walk while talking on the phone.
- Try a fitness app, like a 30-day skipping rope challenge, which is suitable for all fitness levels.
- Pretend you're a boxer and practise throwing some punches in the air. Give the punches some power.
- Try an online yoga session or fitness workout. There are plenty for all fitness levels and tinned food or bottled water can double up for weights.
- Vacuuming, tending to the garden and DIY count too!
- If you have mobility issues, there are lots of seated exercises available online.

It's not selfish to love yourself,
take care of yourself, and to make your
happiness a priority. It's necessary.

MANDY HALE

Exercises to try outdoors:

- Jog or walk briskly around your local area. Whenever possible, get outdoors into nature to help you feel more connected to the world around you.
- Think you can't run? Think again – you absolutely can! Couch to 5K is a fabulous free running plan for beginners, available online or on apps.
- Walk the longer route home and use stairs instead of lifts. Those extra steps make a difference! If you have lunch at your desk, make a conscious effort to pop outside for some fresh air.
- Check your local sports centre – most run classes to suit all abilities and interests. Whether you fancy gentle Pilates, spinning or a weights class, give it a go – you might meet new people too.
- Being in or near water can calm anxiety and bring feelings of ease. Try swimming in a pool or wild-water swimming. Or simply walk near a river and pay attention to the ripples – how does this make you feel?

It's perfectly normal to have days when you've got zero energy and can't even put your trainers on. And that's okay – be kind to yourself and know that it will pass. Let your mind and body rest; you'll soon be recharged to get moving again.

Staying motivated

What exercise can you try each day? Write it here:

Monday	
Tuesday	
Wednesday	
Thursday	
Friday	
Saturday	
Sunday	

Plan your exercise schedule and track your activities using the tracker below. It's a great way to stay motivated and see your progress. Remember to include hydration goals and set weekly targets, like jogging three times or walking to work daily. Consider partnering up with a friend for added support – it makes it fun and it will help them and you!

Goals	
Monday	Activity Duration
Tuesday	Activity Duration
Wednesday	Activity Duration
Thursday	Activity Duration
Friday	Activity Duration
Saturday	Activity Duration
Sunday	Activity Duration

Stay hydrated

Anxiety can cause a dry mouth, tiredness or fogginess, and dehydration can also create these reactions. Not drinking enough water can make anxiety feel worse. Staying hydrated helps to regulate your cortisol (stress hormone) levels and supports overall bodily functions. Aim for eight glasses of water a day.

- Fill a clear bottle with 2 litres of water first thing in the morning and take it with you to drink on the go. You could monitor your water intake by marking the bottle with where you should drink to by 10 a.m., 12 p.m., 2 p.m. etc.
- Sip a glass of water slowly. Pay attention to how you feel. Notice the temperature of the water. Just breathe.
- Jazz up plain water with ginger, mint leaves or lemon juice, or try herbal teas such as camomile or (decaffeinated) green tea.

Alcohol and caffeinated drinks can cause dehydration and amplify jittery feelings, so it's wise to be mindful of your intake. It's common for people to rely on alcohol in social situations to loosen up, but, in the end, this exacerbates anxiety. Try these healthier ways to manage alcohol intake:

- Alternate between an alcoholic drink and a glass of water.
- Create a mocktail you know you'll love. Add a splash of juice, slices of lemon or lime or mint leaves to sparkling water. Enjoy!

Sleep well

Sleeping well is essential for our mental well-being and health. Doesn't everything seem so much brighter after a good night's shut-eye? But when your sleep is broken by anxious thoughts, it can affect your daily functioning.

Golden rules for sleeping well and waking up feeling refreshed

- Set a bedtime and make a habit of going to bed and waking up at the same time every day, including on weekends.
- Have a relaxing bedtime routine to send signals to your mind and body it's time to sleep.
- Avoid caffeine later in the day as it affects your ability to float off to sleep and stay asleep.
- Avoid napping during the day because it can interfere with sleeping at night. If you do nap, make sure it's no longer than 20 minutes.
- Use your bed for sleep only, so your body associates it with time to unwind. Watching TV, looking at your phone or working in bed can make your brain more alert or stressed.
- Make your bedroom relaxing and comfortable. Is it too hot, or too cold? Is it too noisy? Do you need blackout curtains or an eye mask?
- Switch off screens an hour before bedtime because the blue light emitted by devices interrupts the body's natural sleep cycle.
- If you're struggling to fall asleep after 20 minutes, don't try to force it; get out of bed and do a calming activity like meditation or yoga (no screens!).
- Eat well and exercise and your sleep will improve.

Sleep tracker

Ideally, we need 7–9 hours of good quality sleep a night. Use the tracker below to log your sleep patterns for a week. If you notice that you're not sleeping enough or you're waking up feeling tired and negative, make sure you are following the golden rules of sleeping well (page 99) and try the tips to help you relax before bedtime.

Day 1: Morning

Time I went to sleep:	Time I woke up:	Total sleep time:
How did I feel when I woke up? Wide awake, ready to go! ○ Awake, but tired ○ I need more sleep ○		

Day 1: Evening

Number of caffeinated drinks:	I exercised (yes or no):
My mood was...	What I did in the hour before bedtime:

Day 2: Morning

Time I went to sleep:	Time I woke up:	Total sleep time:
How did I feel when I woke up? Wide awake, ready to go! ○ Awake, but tired ○ I need more sleep ○		

Day 2: Evening

Number of caffeinated drinks:	I exercised (yes or no):
My mood was...	What I did in the hour before bedtime:

Day 3: Morning

Time I went to sleep:	Time I woke up:	Total sleep time:
How did I feel when I woke up? Wide awake, ready to go! ○ Awake, but tired ○ I need more sleep ○		

Day 3: Evening

Number of caffeinated drinks:	I exercised (yes or no):
My mood was...	What I did in the hour before bedtime:

Day 4: Morning

Time I went to sleep:	Time I woke up:	Total sleep time:
How did I feel when I woke up? Wide awake, ready to go! ◯ Awake, but tired ◯ I need more sleep ◯		

Day 4: Evening

Number of caffeinated drinks:	I exercised (yes or no):
My mood was...	What I did in the hour before bedtime:

Day 5: Morning

Time I went to sleep:	Time I woke up:	Total sleep time:
How did I feel when I woke up? Wide awake, ready to go! ◯ Awake, but tired ◯ I need more sleep ◯		

Day 5: Evening

Number of caffeinated drinks:	I exercised (yes or no):
My mood was...	What I did in the hour before bedtime:

Day 6: Morning

Time I went to sleep:	Time I woke up:	Total sleep time:
How did I feel when I woke up? Wide awake, ready to go! ◯ Awake, but tired ◯ I need more sleep ◯		

Day 6: Evening

Number of caffeinated drinks:	I exercised (yes or no):
My mood was...	What I did in the hour before bedtime:

Day 7: Morning

Time I went to sleep:	Time I woke up:	Total sleep time:
How did I feel when I woke up? Wide awake, ready to go! ◯ Awake, but tired ◯ I need more sleep ◯		

Day 7: Evening

Number of caffeinated drinks:	I exercised (yes or no):
My mood was...	What I did in the hour before bedtime:

BEDTIME YOGA

We know anxiety and sleep are closely connected. As much as we love to be in the best headspace when we sleep, sometimes it's not entirely possible to be worry-free. Introducing a routine such as bedtime yoga can ensure you're totally relaxed before your head hits the pillow and helps you to float off into tranquillity.

You don't have to be ultra-bendy or super-fit to try yoga – it's for anyone. Research shows yoga has a soothing effect on your body, mind and nervous system. Bedtime yoga in particular can help you achieve a sense of calm before you snooze, so you can wake up feeling revitalized and ready to take on the new day.

Give the simple yoga stretches on the next page a try. Your bed is the best place for doing these rejuvenating yoga poses before you sleep – you'll feel relaxed, and you might even drift off before finishing your practice!

If you haven't tried yoga before, refer to a book or try a free online yoga tutorial.

The present moment is
filled with joy and happiness.
If you are attentive, you will see it.

THÍCH NHẤT HẠNH

Happy baby

Lie on your back, hold on to the soles of your feet, bend your knees and gently push them outwards from your body.

Sleeping butterfly

Lie comfortably on your back. Bring your feet up to bend your knees, then open your knees in a "butterfly" position. Gently relax your hands on your stomach. Take ten long breaths.

Child's pose

Kneel near the edge of your bed, widen your knees, extend your arms and fold over to rest your body on your bed. Take ten deep calm breaths.

Bedtime rituals

Rituals are enjoyable self-care activities that fill us with positive energy. They don't need to be extravagant; even having a bath is a ritual if you're taking time to truly recharge. Here are some activities you can try:

Bathroom rituals

- Take a hot bath an hour or two before bedtime – research shows it drops body temperature by 1 degree Celsius (the ideal temperature to fall asleep).
- Light candles in your bathroom. Wash mindfully – slow it down.
- Sprinkle a little sea salt on a damp face cloth or sponge and softly scrub your face or body, releasing the day's stresses.

Bedroom rituals

- Essential oils have powerful calming effects – they're simple to use for sleep-promoting rituals. Try anxiety-relieving ylang-ylang, mood-lifting bergamot or mind-relaxing lavender. Use diffuser sticks or spritz a few drops on your pillow (or in your bath water).
- Listening to a calming podcast or audiobook can interrupt worrisome thoughts, and a soothing voice helps you fall asleep (it's fabulous mental self-care – like being read a bedtime story!).
- Anxiety often peaks at bedtime, but you can stop niggling worries by imagining locking them away in a worry box and putting them under the bed. Each time a pesky thought pops up, lock it away in the box.
- Journaling your thoughts, hopes and gratitude, or preparing a list for tomorrow, can put your mind at ease.
- Read a book and escape into a captivating story as you drift off.

Bedtime meditation

A relaxation practice before bed can calm the mind, boost restfulness and enhance your sleep quality. Lying down comfortably, close your eyes and take a few deep breaths. As you inhale, feel the oxygen through your body recharging every cell with its fresh energy. With each exhalation, let go of any stress and tension.

Keep breathing deeply and scan your body from head to toe. Notice any pressure, tension or aches. Imagine these feelings melting away with each exhalation.

Continue to breathe and relax a little more deeply. As you do so, let go of any worries. As each worry fades, feel a sense of peace washing over you.

Now imagine yourself on a warm soft mattress of clouds. You're feeling secure, comfortable and supported as the clouds carry you.

Continue breathing slowly, bringing your attention to the top of your head. Imagine a warm golden light filling your head, travelling down your body through your neck and shoulders to your toes and fingers. Feel it nurturing and calming each cell as it fills your body.

Feel the warm light easing any tension and calming your mind. Continue breathing slowly as you release any thoughts and worries with each exhalation. Watch the gold light fade as you float into a deeper sense of calm and relaxation.

You are free and unburdened by any worries right now. You are safe in this moment.

Now that you have let go of your worries, feel the warmth of your bed beneath you and allow yourself to drift off into a peaceful sleep.

LOVE YOURSELF

Many of us struggle to like how we look. Do you cancel plans when you're feeling bad about yourself? How we feel about our body influences our mood and behaviour – a negative body image is linked to social anxiety.

Instead of picking flaws in your appearance, be kinder to and pamper yourself a little – like tending to your skincare or getting a new haircut. Most importantly, shift your focus to feeling grateful for the amazing things your body and mind do for you – your fabulous eyes for allowing you to read, your hands for making warming cups of tea, and your brain for helping you to learn. Write some loving words to yourself using these prompts.

I'm grateful to my body for...

Example: I am grateful to my body for having strong legs to get me from A to B.

....

....

....

....

....

I'm grateful to my mind for...

Example: I'm grateful to my mind for being thoughtful, it helps me to make sound decisions.

....

....

....

....

....

What I love about my character is...

Example: my sense of humour, it makes people smile.

....

....

....

....

....

I'm grateful to be good at...

Example: I'm grateful to be good at working through details; it makes problem-solving easier.

....

....

....

....

....

I'll always remember receiving this compliment...

Example: I'll always remember being told my personality is like a ray of sunshine.

....

....

....

....

....

SOCIAL MEDIA ANXIETY

Social media can be good for connections, but excessive scrolling or worry about posting can increase anxiety. Track your emotions before and after using social media. If it consistently brings negative feelings, take a break.

	Calm	Excited	Annoyed	Sad/envious	Worried
Before					
After					
Before					
After					
Before					
After					
Before					
After					
Before					
After					
Before					
After					
Before					
After					

Within you, there is a stillness and a sanctuary to which you can retreat at any time and be yourself.

HERMANN HESSE

Stay connected

Extensive research spanning decades proves one thing loud and clear: our happiness thrives when we have close relationships. These connections, filled with support and comfort, work wonders on our brains. They empower us to comfort ourselves, just like that friend who's there for us at 2 a.m. after a breakup or the one who effortlessly understands our struggles. Healthy relationships are good medicine – they alleviate anxiety and lift our spirits. That's why it's crucial to stay connected with people who matter. Try this activity:

1. Make a list of people you know well and like spending time with.
2. Next to each name, write when you last saw them.
3. Write down who you'd like to see in the next month and what you might do together.
4. Now get in touch and arrange it!
5. Do this every month.

Name	Last met on...	Activity idea	Met (Y/N)

Practise gratitude

Studies show that practising gratitude is linked to resilience, well-being and positive emotions, which can counteract anxiety and enhance relationships. Each evening, jot down three things you appreciate from your day, like a good meal, a friend's message or the sound of birdsong.

	Three things I am grateful for today		
Monday			
Tuesday			
Wednesday			
Thursday			
Friday			
Saturday			
Sunday			

At the end of the week or when you're feeling low, read through your list of appreciations to remind you how good life is.

Pro tip: **Find reasons throughout the day to thank someone. Make a conscious effort to notice when people are kind to the planet, you or others, and say "thank you".**

Have fun

When you're caught in a frenzy of anxious thoughts, taking time to have fun with friends or family might be the last thing on your mind. But having some downtime helps to release tension. Of course, a light-hearted mindset won't completely melt your worries away, but a little humour helps to get through challenges by making stressful stuff less threatening, and it's totally backed by science! When was the last time you snorted out loud laughing? Try these to have more fun:

- Play a game you loved as a child (it brings those natural feel-good emotions back).
- Watch a comedy that will make your sides ache from laughing.
- Share a joke with friends or co-workers.
- Unleash your creativity – try your hand at art. You don't have to create a masterpiece, just pick up a paintbrush and learn about the different ways to paint, or simply sketch or colour in a colouring book.
- Complete a puzzle. Do one with friends, family or on a date night – it creates togetherness.
- Play board games such as Pictionary, Monopoly or Cluedo – or any game that will promote laughter.
- Download apps to play virtual games – there are plenty of trivia games as well as fantasy ones.

What playful and fun things can you add?

Let nature soothe you

Making time to connect with nature is a wonderful way to relieve your anxiety. It allows you to stay present and it boosts your physical health. Follow these simple ways to let the power of nature soothe you:

- Set yourself a gentle collecting mission on a walk to help you focus on the outside world, taking your attention away from any inner anxieties and worrisome thoughts. Notice leaves, stones, petals, blades of grass, feathers and sticks. Pick things up, notice textures or colours.

- Visit a park or green space. Simply sit on the grass allowing your body to connect with the earth. Let your senses tune into the soundscape around you – the birdsong and sounds of insects. You'll be amazed at what you hear.

- Drawing only requires a piece of paper and a pencil. Get outdoors to focus on sketching an object, such as a tree, or a landscape. Let go of tension as you draw.

- Forest bathing soothes frazzled brains. Find a quiet spot in a forest or green space. Stand or sit against a tree, using your senses to soak in the fresh oxygen, and notice the texture of bark, the trees towering over you, the gentle glow of light and the breeze on your face.

- Journaling or reading a book while sitting on a park bench or in a peaceful garden will help you to appreciate your surroundings. Acknowledge any emotions that surface.

My self-care toolbox

When anxiety strikes, it's easy to forget our helpful tools. That's why it's useful to create your own personalized self-care toolbox. Filling it with go-to calming items prompts you to take a relaxing break and encourages healthy coping mechanisms during stressful times.

Fill an empty box, drawer or container with the things that give you a sense of calm and nourishment. Everyone is unique – fill your box with whatever works for you. What helps to soothe you? Write some ideas down in the space below and include activities you'd like to try in the future too. Here are some ideas to get you started:

- Inspiring books
- Relaxing music
- Photographs of happy memories
- Soothing creative activities: paints, colouring books
- Home spa: scented candles, herbal teas, your favourite chocolate, bubble bath
- For nature lovers: a packet of seeds to grow something or get outdoors
- ....
- ....
- ....
- ....
- ....
- ....
- ....
- ....
- ....

Maybe you could give a relaxation toolbox to a friend in need of calm?

PART 6

Planning
Ahead

Congratulations on persisting in your self-help journey! Always celebrate your wins, no matter how small. Now that you've learned how to take care of yourself effectively, it's important to keep building on your progress.

Life is unpredictable and throws curve balls our way when we least expect it. We might be feeling great, socializing more and watching our anxiety fade away. But sometimes old habits can resurface when we are triggered by something. Imagine meeting a new colleague who gives off similar vibes to someone who was unkind to you. This might activate the social anxiety cycle: your fight-or-flight response, negative thoughts and safety behaviours.

But rest assured, planning and putting strategies in place can help you stay in control so you can manage challenges and deflect anxiousness before it creates a bigger impact on your life. Read on to find out how.

BE PREPARED

When facing anxiety-inducing events like parties, job interviews, dates or presentations, planning and preparation become your trusted allies. Even with the best intentions to look ahead, worrisome thoughts can creep in, leading to procrastination and avoidance of crucial tasks, like accepting party invitations or getting ready for interviews.

In these moments fear takes the reins, whispering "What if I fail?", "What if they don't like me at the party?" or "What if the interviewer senses my nervousness and rejects me?"

The best way to calm your fear response is to create comfort, security and control. This is precisely when solid preparation plays a vital role. Here are some methods to increase your chances of success in the many opportunities that lie before you:

Role-playing

Try role-playing with a trusted person – act out the social situation, such as a job interview, or do a test run of your presentation as if it were really happening. Ask for constructive feedback; you can only do better!

Overcome procrastination

To overcome procrastination, limit distractions, schedule tasks and take action. Don't let social anxiety block your chances. Start making positive changes now for a future you'll appreciate. Get organized, set goals, eliminate distractions and prioritize important tasks.

Prepare your outfit

Decide what you're going to wear at least one day in advance. Make sure it's comfortable and you feel confident in it. Now is not the time to try a new hairstyle or to copy a fashion trend. Stick to what makes you feel amazing!

Plan your logistics

Plan your route, noting parking or public transport options. Keep venue details accessible to avoid last-minute panic. Allow ample travel time and plan a post-event self-care activity, like debriefing with a friend or listening to a calming podcast.

Conversation starters

Ask questions (see page 84) and remember that it's not your sole responsibility to keep conversations going – silence is okay.

   Proper planning will help you feel calm and in control. Don't forget to celebrate your progress afterwards!

Visualization

Visualization is a marvellous tool to add to your self-care toolkit. It helps to lessen anxiety by allowing you to regulate negative emotions and feel relaxed. Essentially, it is a form of meditation that uses your imagination to picture the best possible outcome – you close your eyes and envisage the sights and sounds of a situation playing out like a film with a happy ending.

Visualization is the opposite of what an anxious brain has got used to doing – imagining the worst. Instead of dwelling on the worst-case scenario, visualization lets you explore the best possible outcome before facing social situations, like attending a party where you have an amazing time. If you can picture the worst-case scenario, you can certainly imagine the best-case scenario too!

Imagination is everything.
It is the preview of life's
coming attractions.

ALBERT EINSTEIN

Use visualization to help you rehearse feeling and acting confidently. Practise facing social situations in your imagination first, and then in reality, as follows:

1. Start by imagining a challenging social situation, like meeting new people.

2. Picture as many details as possible. Where are you? What are you doing? Who is around you? Can you hear people laughing? Are they smiling?

3. If you feel a little nervous or self-conscious, that's okay. These feelings will ease the more you practise.

4. Visualize your "confident self". See yourself smiling, calm and relaxed. Feel as powerful as your inner superhero! If negative thoughts pop up, like "This is silly", say "Goodbye, I'm busy saving myself and getting stronger."

5. Take a mental snapshot of this self-assured, empowered you and allow your inner confidence to grow.

6. Any time you face an anxiety-provoking situation, recall this mental snapshot of the confident you.

You are stronger and more capable than you might realize!

Daily visualization

The more time you dedicate to visualization, the stronger your sense of confidence will become. Embrace this practice as a daily ritual to reprogram your brain with positive patterns. Start immersing yourself in visualizing everything through a positive lens – you'll become just as good at imagining the best outcomes as you have been at visualizing negative ones. You might even find yourself looking forward to things that worried you!

If you need inspiration for cultivating confidence, jot down the qualities and traits you admire in people who navigate social situations effortlessly, or watch videos showcasing your favourite icons exuding confidence. Use the techniques you have learned from the previous sections – affirmations, power-posing or knowing your strengths – to propel yourself towards your goals.

Picture this scenario: you're at a party and anxiety strikes unexpectedly. Instead of slipping back into old habits, imagine yourself standing confidently on a stage, transcending the anxious feeling.

Get SMART

As you've seen, anxiety and procrastination often go together, making even simple tasks feel daunting. To tackle big goals, break them into smaller, manageable steps. SMART goal-setting is key, enabling you to create specific, measurable, achievable goals. Here's an example:

Specific	I aim to increase time spent communicating with a family member and a close friend by 15 minutes per day. This will help overcome social anxiety and improve my social skills.
Measurable	I will track each conversation I have with a friend or family member and mark it on a calendar.
Achievable	I will start with shorter conversations and gradually work my way up to 15 minutes as I become more comfortable.
Relevant	This goal is relevant because lack of human contact is not good for me and makes my social anxiety worse. Practising regular conversations with friends and family can help me build confidence.
Time-bound	I will commit to this goal for the next month and re-evaluate my progress at the end of that period.

My SMART goals

Use the chart below to help you set some SMART goals for each month. You can use this goal-setting technique for the anxiety staircase on page 82 to help you get started.

S	What do you **specifically** want to achieve?
M	How will you **measure** success?
A	What do you need to help you **achieve** it?
R	Is your goal **realistic**?
T	How much **time** do you need to achieve this goal?

Monthly reflections

At the end of each month, review and reflect on your progress.

Monthly reflection

Things I loved about last month:

....

Things I am grateful for:

....

Next month I could improve:

....

	Goal	Action steps	Do by (date)	✔
Week 1				
Week 2				
Week 3				
Week 4				

Monthly reflection

Things I loved about last month:

....

....

Things I am grateful for:

....

....

Next month I could improve:

....

....

	Goal	Action steps	Do by (date)	✔
Week 1				
Week 2				
Week 3				
Week 4				

Monthly reflection

Things I loved about last month:

....

....

Things I am grateful for:

....

....

Next month I could improve:

....

....

	Goal	Action steps	Do by (date)	✔
Week 1				
Week 2				
Week 3				
Week 4				

PART 7

Being True
to Yourself

In the previous chapter, you learned about the importance of planning ahead to tackle unexpected challenges like speaking in front of a group or attending a big social gathering. These strategies are a great way to stop you falling into the social anxiety trap when you're mixing with others, but it's equally, if not more, crucial to stay authentic and true to yourself during these interactions.

Let's face it, there's nothing worse than going through the motions of life just for the sake of it. Hiding parts of yourself or pretending to be someone else not only drains your energy but also chips away at your self-esteem and confidence. That's why it's time to build on all the progress you've made so far on your self-improvement journey and fully embrace your authentic self. You don't have to try to fit in, you are incredible just as you are! Keep reading to discover how to stay true to yourself.

Be yourself

Everyone wants to feel seen, heard, validated and like they belong – it's an innate human instinct. So surely a little edit of ourselves can't hurt if it means we get to belong? The truth is, not showing up fully as you are causes problems in the long run, as you lose your self-worth and sense of who you are. Also, people can tell when someone is not being authentic, which can impact the chances of making genuine connections.

Being yourself means being true to your own values, beliefs and personality, rather than conforming to the expectations of others. It sounds easier said than done, right? Sometimes it's hard to just be yourself. Many of us struggle because often we hide parts of ourselves we might feel ashamed of, or it's easier to slip into a certain role to "fit in".

We can only truly be ourselves when we feel comfortable in our own skin. That means accepting all our imperfections (we all have them) and our appearance, and being content with where we are in life. Yes, it takes courage, but being your most authentic self will free you from the pressure and anxiety of trying to follow the crowd. It's time to embrace your unique and amazing individuality.

When you are content to be simply yourself and don't compare or compete, everyone will respect you.

LAO TZU

My values

To be true to yourself, start by understanding your values. Values are what you treasure in life, such as kindness or equality. They are powerful as they shape your goals, priorities and identity. Staying true to what matters to you helps you embrace your authentic self.

Circle the values that matter most to you.

Leadership
Creativity
Toughness
Friendship
Curiosity
Adaptability
Cautiousness
Rationality
Helpfulness
Determination
Honesty
Sociability
Adventurousness
Cleanliness
Patience
Liveliness
Empathy
Happiness
Kindness
Freedom
Intellect
Achievement
Excitement
Equality
Wisdom
Loyalty
Self-control
Bravery
Modesty
Independence
Organization
Gratitude
Optimism
Love
Imagination
Well-being of my family

LET GO OF EXPECTATIONS

Have you ever felt obliged to "look the part", dress a certain way, find "the one", be a homeowner or have a "perfect body"? Sadly, these annoying expectations are placed on us by family, media, social media or friends. Sometimes we place unrealistic expectations on ourselves too by striving for perfection in everything.

When you're under this type of daily pressure, thoughts about "not being good enough" when measured against these expectations only make your anxiety worse.

What pressure or expectations do you feel from your friends, family, work, the media or other sources? Jot them down here:

....

....

....

....

....

....

....

....

....

....

....

....

....

....

Some expectations are healthy and can encourage you to do better, even if they're burdensome – like working long hours to get promoted. But this is your aspiration, so it's a choice, whereas some external pressures aren't helpful, especially if they're unattainable.

Think about which expectations are helpful to you. Which expectations are unhelpful to you? What would it be like to let go of them?

What expectations are unhelpful?

....

....

....

....

....

....

....

What unhelpful expectations do you have of yourself?

....

....

....

....

....

....

....

Accept yourself

Most of us look to other people for approval and acceptance – it's human nature. The problem is, when your self-worth is in the hands of someone else, it makes anxiety worse.

When you accept yourself and trust your own opinion of who you are more than the opinions of others, anxiety starts to vanish.

Self-acceptance is being self-compassionate rather than comparing yourself to other people and then berating yourself for not measuring up. Inner talk like "I should be perfect" and "I should be outgoing" needs to be replaced with much kinder language. Here are some examples, with space to add your own:

I can be a work in progress and still be enough.	I am happy with where I am.
I accept who I am, even though I may not like some of my traits.	I am perfect just as I am, even when facing criticism.

When social anxiety takes hold, it's like a camera lens zooming in, fixating (often excessively) on minor details like "They're laughing, it must be about me." To overcome this, zoom out from what you can't control – such as others' reactions – and shift your focus to what you can control. It's your most valuable ally.

Here are some things we can and cannot control. Add your own:

Things we can't control

Whether people accept me

What people say about me

How others feel about me

When others act negatively

What people think about me

Whether others appreciate my good qualities

Things we can control

My own self-talk

Finding the courage to try new things

Accepting others as they are

Passing over negative thoughts

Accepting myself as I am

How I react to criticism

Choosing to love myself

Set clear boundaries

To reduce social anxiety, know your limits and set boundaries. Focus on what's important and let go of anxiety-inducing obligations. For example, helping a friend shouldn't mean sacrificing your own well-being.

Remember, relationships are two-way – your needs matter too! Learn how to assert yourself (page 80) and set clear boundaries. People who care will be willing to accommodate your needs. Get comfortable with boundary-setting language. Add your own statements to the table below:

I'm not comfortable with this.	Please don't do that.	I need some space right now.
Sorry, not this time.	I can't do that for you.	I've changed my mind.

When it's not practical to verbalize your needs, you can use body language to communicate discomfort instead – and simply leave if you ever feel unsafe.

Trust

Social anxiety has kept you confined, instilling in you a fear of people and social situations by convincing you they are unsafe. This fear leaves you feeling small and helpless, and leads to avoiding interactions. The best remedy for fear is trust.

When you start socializing, attending events or trying the anxiety staircase experiments, it's natural to feel a little scared. Place trust in yourself, the process and the individuals you engage with. Of course, trust inherently carries risk, but it also presents opportunities for connection and happy moments.

Building trust takes time and requires a balance between caution and openness to new experiences. The truth is, not everyone is threatening. You can begin to build healthy relationships and learn to trust that others can love and accept you, flaws and all.

Do what you were born to do. You just have to trust yourself.

BEYONCÉ

Healthy relationships

Every relationship, whether it is with a sibling, friend or romantic partner, is unique. Healthy relationships share positive qualities, like those in the green flags list below. Unhealthy relationships usually carry negative qualities, like in the red flags list below. Are there any qualities you might add?

Red flags	Green flags
Ignores your messages	Replies to your messages
Lies to you	Is open and honest with you
Is unsupportive of your goals	Supports you
Controls who you see or what you wear	Allows you to be yourself
Is critical of you and puts you down	Compliments and builds you up
Gets jealous when things go well for you	Feels happy for you when things go well
Breaks your trust	Can be trusted with personal information
Only calls when they need something	Calls to see how you are – they care
Doesn't care about your feelings	Is kind and considerate of your feelings
Creates drama	Creates stability and feelings of safety

It's important to take a step back from our relationships and reflect on whether they are nourishing or depleting us. Use these prompts to reflect on your relationships.

Who is the first one to reach out most of the time?

....

....

How much have I opened up to them? How do I feel about this?

....

....

What are my favourite and least favourite things about them?

....

....

On a scale of one to ten how comfortable am I around them?

....

....

How long do I expect the relationship or friendship to last? How do I feel about it?

....

....

If a relationship is harming your mental health, removing yourself from it can sometimes be the healthiest option. Remember to stay close to people who want more for you not from you.

PART 8

Looking
Forward

Social anxiety can feel like you're adrift in deep water with no land in sight. It might seem like the future is all gloomy and devoid of hope, but guess what? It doesn't have to be that way.

You've already shown incredible bravery by taking important steps from this workbook to break free from the grip of social anxiety. Congratulations! It's important to recognize your own strength and know that you CAN create a brighter future. Armed with the tools and skills you've acquired, you can be socially confident and embrace a new chapter in your life.

So, in this last part, let's explore what comes next on this journey of overcoming social anxiety and looking forward to better days. You've learned so much along the way, and now it's time to put it all into practice. Let's do this!

A brighter future

Working towards a brighter future requires making these key changes:

- Stay hopeful and remember you are not alone. So many people have overcome social anxiety and are living fulfilling lives. You can too!

- Know your strengths and play to them. You're not defined by past mistakes. It's time to move forward.

- Your thoughts are not facts. Be your own superhero and call them out before you get sucked into a social anxiety rut.

- Don't forget, you are in control. You have a safety plan that reminds you about using healthy coping strategies, the importance of talking to someone, and your reasons to stay hopeful.

- Give yourself a chance and stop getting in your own way by being fairer and kinder and showering yourself with self-compassion. Remember, if you wouldn't speak to a friend in that way then don't say it to yourself.

- Keep experimenting with different social situations and interactions then reflect – the only way to improve is by putting yourself out there. You can do it and one day you might be able to help someone overcome their fears too (imagine how rewarding that will feel).

- Identify your values and be true to yourself. This way you can set healthy boundaries and make nourishing connections with people.

- Set goals and figure out how to achieve them. Don't forget to celebrate your progress!

- And finally, look after yourself – use your self-care toolbox to live a healthy life.

You are not alone

Please remember social anxiety affects more people than you might realize; you're certainly not alone. Social settings and interactions are a source of anxiety for many people, even those who come across confidently can experience anxiety in social situations.

Numerous celebrities, such as Kim Basinger, Nicole Kidman, Naomi Osaka, Jennifer Lawrence, Ricky Williams, Barbra Streisand and Adele, have opened up about their struggles with social anxiety. They are living proof that you can live your life in the face of anxiety. When socializing, if you're worried about being judged, remember others feel the same.

Support groups are also a great reminder that you're not the only one living with social fears. A lot of people you encounter feel the same way, and you certainly don't have to suffer in silence.

Talk about it

Social anxiety is especially tough when it's a silent battle. Perhaps you don't want to burden people, or you feel no one will understand. But this is not the case: there's always someone who will listen in confidence.

To really move through social anxiety, you need to talk about it. Feeling understood is important, so try opening up to a close friend or family member. Or, if it feels more comfortable, talk to a therapist or doctor.

Sharing your emotions sheds light in dark times and you'll be surprised by the support and reassurance people lend. For instance, if you tell someone your anxiety is triggered by large family gatherings, they won't take it personally if you miss the next one. Use this space to write down what you'd like to say.

My anxiety is triggered by...

....

....

....

....

....

You could help me by...

....

....

....

....

....

Future goals vision board

Setting goals for a brighter future is always a good idea, especially ones you can visualize. By creating a vision board, you can include images, inspiring quotes and affirmations as well as the steps you need to take to achieve a goal. Remember, visualization is powerful! It is super motivating, boosts your mood and can help you to succeed.

Whether your goal is related to your career, health or hobbies, use a goals vision board to start small or dream big. Track your progress visually too – get as creative as you wish.

Goal (e.g. hiking in a new area with a friend):

....

....

....

Date: ....

What steps do I need to take to make it happen (e.g. set dates, find route, walking gear)?

....

....

....

....

....

....

....

Visualization board (e.g. inspiring quotes, affirmations, magazine cut-outs, postcards, doodles):

What's in your box?

Here's a reminder of some of the tools we've explored so you can show anxiety the door and feel calmer and in control. Which ones will you choose to put in your mental toolbox? Jot your answers down alongside the suggestions.

Stay hopeful – page 23

Daily breathing – page 36

Get creative – page 39

Move my body – page 40

Thought catching – page 52

Best possible outcome – page 58

Focus on socializing – page 68

Strike a power pose – page 75

Face my fears – page 82

Set SMART goals – page 122

Healthy relationships – page 136

MY SAFETY PLAN

Your safety plan serves as a personalized collection of coping strategies that work for you. On those tough days when you're struggling, rely on this plan as a gentle reminder to nudge you in the right direction. Following the steps should lower your anxiety levels. So, no matter how overwhelmed you feel, rest assured that your plan exists to restore your sense of safety.

I know I am triggered when I notice...

....

....

....

....

Some good ways to distract myself are... (e.g. podcast, visualization, movie)

....

....

....

....

Some activities that soothe me are... (e.g. colouring, brisk walk)

....

....

....

....

Coping skills I can use are... (e.g. breathing exercises, affirmations)

. . . .

. . . .

. . . .

. . . .

My reasons to be grateful...

1. . . . .

2. . . . .

3. . . . .

4. . . . .

Safe people I can call are... (e.g. friend, family member)

. . . .

. . . .

. . . .

. . . .

Other resources I can turn to are... (e.g. support group, books, professional help)

. . . .

. . . .

. . . .

. . . .

BOOST YOUR CONFIDENCE

Embracing new challenges will help to boost your social confidence and prevent you slipping back into old habits. Engaging in hobbies or causes, even if they initially feel a little scary, shifts your focus away from yourself and towards a broader purpose. Venturing out into the community and joining clubs offers a wonderful opportunity to combat loneliness. Here are some ideas to consider:

- Join a public speaking group like Toastmasters to improve your communication skills and gain confidence in public speaking.
- Take dance classes such as salsa, Bollywood or Zumba to develop social ease through physical movement and have fun in the process.
- Volunteer for a cause close to your heart, like helping at a soup kitchen, and experience the uplifting "helper's high". As well as fostering a sense of belonging, this leads to the satisfaction of contributing your time to a worthy cause.
- Join a book club or cycling club, take yoga classes or cookery lessons, or explore any other interest you enjoy. You'll get to engage with like-minded individuals and build connections.
- Attend community events like festivals or concerts to mingle with people in a relaxed social environment.

By actively participating in these activities, you prove self-doubt wrong, build self-esteem and unlock new-found social confidence.

Keep pushing yourself to find new ways of overcoming your anxiety. Make a list of situations that still scare you or cause you anxiety and take your time to tackle them one by one. Write them down here:

....

....

....

....

....

....

....

....

....

....

....

....

....

....

....

....

....

....

....

....

Building social confidence takes time, so be patient and celebrate your successes. Remember to seek support from trusted friends, or professionals if needed. You're doing amazingly! Keep going!

Alternative therapies

If you're interested in nurturing your mind–body connection to alleviate anxiety, alternative therapies offer a potential answer. Treatments like acupuncture, acupressure, aromatherapy and herbal remedies can be used alongside traditional treatments, such as medication, CBT, psychotherapy or counselling, or as standalone alternatives.

However, alternative therapies alone might not be enough, especially if you're experiencing significant disruptions in your daily life. Always consult your doctor before trying a new therapy.

Acupuncture, a form of Chinese medicine, uses fine needles to stimulate specific areas of the body, releasing blocked energy and activating the nervous system to ease conditions like anxiety, headaches and digestive issues. **Acupressure** achieves similar results but uses pressure instead of needles. Apply firm pressure to these points for a few minutes:

Shen Men is at the tip of the triangle-like hollow in your upper ear. Stimulate this to relieve anxiety, stress and insomnia.

Close your eyes, take deep breaths and massage **Yin Tang** for 5 minutes to release tension and calm anxiousness (it's halfway between your eyebrows).

Inner Frontier Gate is between the two tendons on your forearm, three finger widths beneath your wrist. Massage it to reduce anxiety or ease nausea and pain.

Aromatherapy uses essential oils to promote body relaxation and mental tranquillity. Lavender is widely popular for its anxiety-calming and sleep-inducing properties. Try:

- Inhaling the scent by adding a few drops to your bath, handkerchief, diffuser or pillow mist
- Blending lavender essential oil with body lotion and applying it to your skin
- Using dried lavender to make a tea or liquid extract

Herbal remedies can aid in alleviating mild to moderate anxiety, although research is ongoing. They boost overall well-being and mental health. Explore these options:

- **Rhodiola rosea (golden root or arctic root):** an adaptogen that boosts stress resistance
- **St John's wort:** a popular herbal supplement for mild to moderate depression and increasingly used for anxiety reduction
- **Valerian root:** used for centuries to address sleep issues, digestive disorders and nervous tension
- **Ashwagandha (Indian ginseng or winter cherry):** enhances resilience to physical and emotional stress

Yoga extends beyond exercise, as studies highlight its ability to nurture the mind–body connection and promote inner serenity through mindful movements and breathing techniques. It complements CBT effectively. Try online yoga videos or consider attending in-person classes.

SEEKING PROFESSIONAL HELP

If social anxiety is impacting your life, it might be a good idea to seek help from a doctor or mental health professional, or to reach out to organizations to give yourself the best chance of recovery. Remember, there is absolutely no shame in asking for help – it is a sign of strength and there are people who want to listen. You don't have to suffer alone.

Anxiety UK

03444 775 774 (helpline)
07537 416 905 (text)
www.anxietyuk.org.uk
Anxiety UK offers support and advice for people living with anxiety.

Mind

0300 123 3393 (helpline)
www.mind.org.uk
Mind has support pages, information, videos, an online community and self-care tips for living with social anxiety. There's an interactive crisis page with practical advice to help you cope.

YoungMinds

0808 802 5544 (helpline for parents)
Text "SHOUT" to 85258 (text support for young people)
www.youngminds.org.uk
YoungMinds aims to stop young people's mental health reaching crisis point, including those from diverse communities. Young people share their tips and real-life stories on coping with social anxiety. Resources for parents and schools are included too.

Anxiety & Depression Association of America

www.adaa.org
This is a charity that aims to improve the quality of life of those with anxiety disorders.

Mental Health America

www.mhanational.org
Text "MHA" to 741741 to connect with a trained crisis counsellor.
If you just need to talk to someone, but are not in crisis, consider reaching out to a warmline on mhanational.org/warmlines. The organization offers advice and support for mental health and has links to online communities.

Samaritans

UK call 116 123 / www.samaritans.org
USA call 1 (800) 273-TALK / samaritansusa.org
Whatever you're going through, contact the Samaritans for support. This is a 24/7 confidential and non-judgemental listening service. If you prefer to write about how you are feeling, you can email jo@samaritans.org.

Conclusion

Congratulations on starting your self-help journey. Hopefully, you will now know that you are not alone. Many of us struggle with social anxiety, but plenty have overcome it — even if they don't always choose to talk about their journeys.

Now you have a better understanding of social anxiety, you have the power to overcome it too. Each step you take forward is a sign you're not willing to give up on yourself. Even doing something as seemingly simple as flicking through the pages of this book is powerful.

Your confidence will soar when you find the courage to address the problem. Your eyes will open wide to see new perspectives on your life and the possibilities ahead of you. Your struggles will get easier, and you will create more opportunities to make meaningful connections. Social interactions will gradually become more comfortable. If you have a bad day, that's okay — every day is a new start. Over time, you will feel less anxious and more connected.

Choose to trust everything will work out as the best-case scenario. Take this hope with you as you keep moving forward. Most importantly, you can't control the approval of others but you can take steps to be the authority of joy in your life. **You can do this!**

Resources

The following resources are in addition to those on pages 152–153. They might give you extra support, comfort or inspiration on your well-being journey.

Books

Edmund J. Bourne, *The Anxiety and Phobia Workbook* (2020)
Joshua Fletcher, *Anxiety: Panicking about Panic: A Powerful, Self-Help Guide for Those Suffering from an Anxiety or Panic Disorder* (2014)
Shad Helmstetter, PhD, *Negative Self-Talk & How to Change It* (2019)
Chris Macleod, MSW, *The Social Skills Guidebook: Manage Shyness, Improve Your Conversations, and Make Friends, Without Giving Up Who You Are* (2016)
Glenn R Schiraldi, PhD, *The Self-Esteem Workbook* (2017)

Websites

Here are some useful links to websites showcasing helpful information, advice and tools on social anxiety and mental health:
www.aboutsocialanxiety.com
www.socialanxietyinstitute.org
www.succeedsocially.com
www.nhs.uk/mental-health (UK)
www.ecouch.com.au (Australia)
www.anxietycanada.com (Canada)
www.psychcentral.com/anxiety/social-anxiety-disorder-symptoms (USA)

Podcasts

Your Social Anxiety Bestie with Sadie Hall
Voted the best podcast by psychcentral.com for anyone who struggles with social interactions

Social Anxiety Solutions - Your Journey to Social Confidence!
Interviews with "the superstars of the therapy and psychology world", with specific action steps

The Calmer You Podcast
Insightful tips on coping with anxiety and silencing your inner critic

Get Sleepy
Rated the number one sleep podcast on Spotify, with stories and meditations to help "calm the mind and relax the body"

Mindset Change (UK)
Reset your mindset to change your life using a "holistic blend of psychology, hypnosis, neurobiology, NLP, psychotherapy tools and strategies"

Support groups, communities, online forums

UK-based social anxiety discussion board – social-anxiety.org.uk
US-based social anxiety support discussion board – socialanxietysupport.com
Social phobia world discussion board – socialphobiaworld.com

Charities

No Panic (UK) – nopanic.org (search for "social anxiety" to access the informative blog and tips)
Social Anxiety Association (USA) – socialphobia.org
ReachOut (under 25s, Australia) – au.reachout.com
Mental Health Foundation (UK) – mentalhealth.org.uk

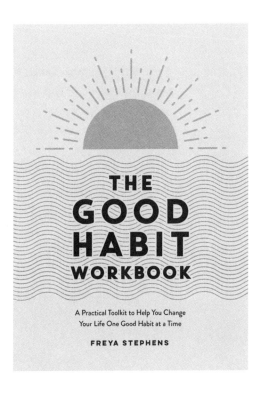

The Good Habit Workbook

A Practical Toolkit to Help You Change Your Life One Good Habit at a Time

Freya Stephens

Paperback

978-1-83799-028-3

Habits are the building blocks of our days, and they have a huge impact on how we live – they affect what we do, how we feel and the paths in life that we choose to take.

The Good Habit Workbook contains practical advice, effective tips and guided exercises based on trusted cognitive behavioural therapy (CBT) techniques. It will help you to break free from negative cycles that aren't serving you and replace them with positive, productive habits for long-term health and happiness.

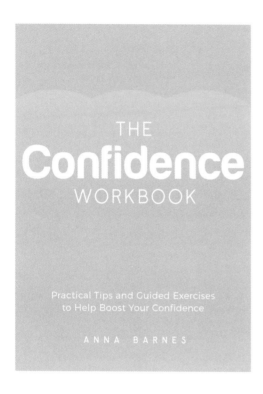

The Confidence Workbook

Practical Tips and Guided Exercises to Help Boost Your Confidence

Anna Barnes

Paperback

978-1-80007-715-7

Life can be challenging, and it's normal to feel unsure of yourself sometimes. But when low self-confidence becomes a regular occurrence and you start avoiding certain situations because of it, it's time to find a strategy to start believing in yourself.

The Confidence Workbook contains practical tips, thoughtful advice and guided exercises to help you overcome self-doubt. Based on trusted mindfulness techniques, this workbook will fill you with the assurance you need to become your own cheerleader and focus on the things you really like about the person in the mirror.

Image credits

Have you enjoyed this book? If so, find us on Facebook at
Summersdale Publishers, on Twitter/X at @Summersdale
and on Instagram and TikTok at @summersdalebooks
and get in touch. We'd love to hear from you!

www.summersdale.com